Movies in Society

(Sex, Crime and Censorship)

MOVIES IN SOCIETY

(SEX, CRIME AND CENSORSHIP)

by

MARK KOENIGIL

ROBERT SPELLER & SONS, PUBLISHERS, INC.
33 WEST 42ND STREET
NEW YORK 36

FIRST EDITION

PRINTED IN THE UNITED STATES OF AMERICA
BY CHARLES PRESS, INC.

DEDICATION

I dedicate this book to *Dr. João Belchior Marques Goulart*, PRESIDENT OF BRAZIL, whom I consider my friend, and to the BRAZILIAN MOTION PICTURE INDUSTRY, in hope that the observations in this book may help to put it on its feet.

TABLE OF CONTENTS

LIST OF ILLUSTRATIONS

viii

Mexican film—	THE VAGABOND (*Vagabundo*)
German Sex-Education Film:—	TOMORROW I WILL BE A WOMAN (*Vom Madchen Zur Frau*)
Film on which author collaborated:—	THE LADY FROM MAXIM'S (*French*)
Technical stereotypes:—	DUEL CLOSE-UP (*American Plan*)
Types of mass-appeal films:—	Nudist — War — Western — Tarzan Sex — Horror — Bedroom Farce Juvenile Delinquency
Censored Films of Controversy:—	FOREVER AMBER LADY CHATTERLEY'S LOVER MARTIN LUTHER GARDEN OF EDEN

Prologue

Some of the foreign titles in this book are literal translations, others have meanings which we think are more appropriate in their definition. There is greater opportunity for this especially in the chapter on the Brazilian Movie where some of the titles were never shown in any English-speaking nation. It is sometimes very difficult to translate from Portuguese into English and still retain the same meaning. On many occasions the translation is almost impossible and the interpretation may suffer. In any event all translations of foreign films serve a purpose and give the reader familiar with a foreign language the approximate meaning in their native tongue.

We are indebted to all major studios and distributors for their information and stills which illustrate this book—among them:—Twentieth Century Fox, M.G.M., Universal International, Paramount, Lux Films, Columbia Pictures, Lopert Films, Warner Brothers, Harrison Films, United Artists, Allied Artists, Louis de Rochemont Films, Kingsley International, Continental Films and many others that were kind enough to give their time and knowledge to help me write this work.

My special gratitude goes to Mrs. Maria de Freitas Treen, of the College of the City of New York (Adult Extension Division), who patiently translated and typed numerous pages and edited many of the chapters of this book.

I am also grateful to Mr. Jon Speller and Mr. Robert Speller for giving their time and help in editing and discussing with me different chapters of this book. They enabled me to publish my work in the United States, in the English language.

My thanks also to Bill Everson, British movie critic and writer, for collaboration on the chapter on American movies and his professional advice and corrections. And to all whom

I may have failed to mention, to all the others for their help in accumulating information in the United States, France and Brazil, and particularly to the Johnson Office, M.P.A.A., the Brazilian Consulate General in New York, the Brazilian Government Trade Bureau and Mr. Alvaro Lins and Mr. Manuel Bandeira, members of the Brazilian Academy of Letters for encouragement and for awarding me the National Prize of Brazil in 1955—the "Carlos de Laet" Award for the presentation of my work in its original version.

I have written this book in the sincere hope that people all over the world will acquire a better understanding of motion picture problems and to present to the American public for the first time a clear picture of the Brazilian motion picture industry with the hope that an interest to see some of the fine Brazilian films may be awakened.

In this work I am trying to encompass various new sociological, criminal and sexual approaches and facets in the cinema which previous to this have not been presented to the public in a realistic manner.

My appendix includes a brief study of the Brazilian movie industry as well as my speech to the Brazilian Congress which accompanied a project—to create a Special Association to control the Brazilian Motion Picture Industry along national and international lines—presented to the President, who in turn submitted it to the Congress for further study.

Introduction

Chapter 1

INTRODUCTION—Part A
THE CINEMA AND ITS INFLUENCE

The spectator sitting in darkness before the motion picture screen, from the psychological point of view, becomes a slave.✓ He is made to project, think and reflect in a cinematic world that is well-defined; reactions to the fictitious and imaginative elements depend to a great extent on his temperament, sensibility, education and social position. All this determines his response to the film from which he may adopt good or bad examples.

Therein lies the cumulative power and the extent of good influences or the grave psychic danger of the cinema, television and other newer types of media such as 3D, etc. The motion picture message is notable in the fact that men are differentiated in their reactions into various types of groupings. Cohen-Seat has said in his book *Notions Fundamentales et Vocabulaire de Filmologie* that the element of escape from emotional reality plays an important role in movie-going.

On occasion the films will reveal the nature of a people, its civilization, its ideals, its basic political and religious problems, as well as its dogmatic ideas.

The most intense pathological impact of a film is found ∨ in scenes of great contrast and violent emotions, such as in scenes of very pronounced eroticism involving partial or complete nudity, violence and killings which can later be imitated by the viewer.

Needless to say, the cinematic action will be aped by a very susceptible and nervous individual, or one under the influence of alcohol or one who is weak and apt to commit

5

irrational acts. Some intelligent people will brush off such a reaction with the comment "he had an inferiority complex" but actually—what is an inferiority complex? It would be difficult to say clearly; some will say "he had perverse inclinations, he is psychopathic or just another crazy fellow."

The truth is much simpler. He is sick. But we are all sick; some more, others, less. The revealed or hidden sickness is brought forth in the individual by different circumstances in life: by the phenomena of war, bombings, concentration camps, loss of parents and loved ones, personal sensibilities, a sensitive intellect or any personal crisis.

In our daily work, which is more or less routine, any unexpected occurrence such as a great misfortune, a period of alcoholism, a great unfulfilled desire and many other factors can bring about a pathological state in the cases of weak individuals, regardless of race, color, or creed. If there are exceptions in this category, I am not aware of them.

In accordance with their adaptive or natural reflexes, they will react to the influence of a definite media—such as the cinema: there are others, but let us discuss the field that interests us which is the cinema and derivative media.

Producers, critics and fans, all realize that the best films are those that contain fragments from daily life. Some realistic films have become great successes. In showing the poor how the rich live, the movies concentrate on a very small segment of society: the very privileged class. The danger of being influenced by the cinema is much less to the wealthy members of society and members of the middle-class, than to those in the lower echelons. The more compassionate members of the privileged class may show some sign of torment, utter a few words of regret, or shudder at scenes of misery but without any real personal conviction. Perhaps on leaving the cinema they will give a coin to a beggar in the belief that thus they are alleviating the misery of the world. Others will have no reaction whatsoever.

The cinema invariably has the same themes with little variation: the strongest always win, justice always triumphs, crime does not pay. The capitalist with his full purse (he is the favorite) is the winner in reality as well as in the movies. We can say that life is a kind of cinema of mankind. It is filmed by an invisible machine. Time passes, life ends. Daily happenings set the stage of each passing day and each may play his own part. There are no spectators here—or better still, each "artist" assumes a triple role; he is the author, the principal hero and the spectator. At the same time, he is a judge of himself and of others, and is therefore the only judge (to himself) of any occurrence or crime committed.

Many times this justice errs but few such cases are known to us. It is said that in the heavens there is a Supreme Judge. At least, that is what every religion teaches and that every man will receive his just due sooner or later. All are satisfied with that. What else can they do! Mankind has found different ways to take a man's life but has not yet discovered a way to give it back to him—only to prolong it perhaps, but even then not always with success.

There are producers who believe that by showing spectators films on social injustice, errors on the part of governments, and miscarriages of justice, they will then benefit mankind, but they are absolutely wrong. The effects are counterproductive. The immature audiences come to the wrong conclusion: the semi-literate and the poor being unable to delve deeply into the matter become antagonistic to the wealthy classes, commenting among themselves that there is no justice for the poor.

Others say "When I become rich, I can do anything, thus—why should I be poor if it is so easy to become rich?" as they see depicted on the screen. If there is a mistake, it is the poor man who suffers—but to become rich any manner is justifiable and all to the good. For this category of people, the movies represent the greatest influence on their actions.

Tentative attempts have been made to employ the film as a therapeutic device in the Hospital for "Children with Mental Diseases" in Paris. This program is directed by Professor Heuyer, great French psychologist and criminologist.

This is what the famous French specialist has said:

"The film is a means of transforming the world. What does it tell us? The danger that may result to the viewer and society in general is greater than the danger that an industry might suffer by the loss of some profits. One should take precautions with regard to images that move. On them depend victory and calamity. They produce virtue or dishonesty, slothfulness or vigor, sublime quality or depravity. As Aesop said:

"The best or the worst will triumph."

In Alexandre Arnoux's book *Du muet au parlant,* Lucien Descaves, one of the pioneers of the cinema, is quoted:

"We allowed the children to go to the cinema, now the time has come for the cinema to come to the children."

After a half century of existence the cinema has acquired a facility of expression which allows it to attack the most difficult social and psychological subjects. We have seen films based on the most intricate themes, such as the demoralization of a nation by anonymous letters, life in an old-age asylum, the destruction brought by the war and its consequences on youth, the "photocopies" of daily crimes practiced by young delinquents and adults who in the majority have as a basis for their crimes eroticism and poverty.

We allow ourselves in this manuscript to cite the different crimes committed in the whole world, provoked by the images that move, and to those people, that is the only significance the cinema has. The cinema has developed such a potency in evocation and analysis that it is not arbitrary to compare it to the more ancient arts, like the theatre, romance and poetry.

The cinema due to its need for varied subject matter was

forced to seek more and more material for the sake of originality and prosperity in the rich fields of science, including psychology and psychiatry. Rene Barjavel in his book *Total Cinema* tells us: "It is proper to recognize that the cinema has in the life of a nation twenty centuries old, a considerably greater place than the theatre and literature."

One feels profound enthusiasm for the cinema—in fact, one works for it, not always for the value that it can give us but rather for that which it allows us.

We like the cinema in general, when the films are good, but not when we see that films for adults are viewed by children to the detriment of the latter.

Subjects such as romance, the problems of prostitution, the origins of crime, and sexual eroticism are easily absorbed by adolescents, increasing their nervousness, their hidden sadism, the energy and the totality of their basic emotions. It places them in a state of supressed nervousness.

In the greater number of the cases, the young people try to explore in real life scenes shown on the screen which almost invariably lead into grave episodes whether they be social or criminal, and in their culminating phases are felt sooner or later in the social strata to which they belong.

If we consider, for example, the film showings on one afternoon in Paris, without judging in advance the content of the films, we could see such titles as *La Scandaleuse de Berlin* (The Shameful Girl from Berlin) *Au delà des grilles* (Beyond the Bars), *Nous sommes tous des assassins* (We are all Murderers) *La P. Respectueuse,* (The Respectful Prostitute) *Le Crime Parfait* (The Perfect Crime) etc. Brazilian newspapers in Rio de Janiero and São Paulo advertise titles like *Cry of the City, The Asphalt Jungle,* the 'Western type' like *Marshall of Amarillo, The Justice of the Range,* a pirate film such as *Treasure Island,* etc.—all made in America since the Brazilian Movie Industry does not produce detective films and much less pirate films or Westerns.

If we go to the cinema in Mexico, Italy or Spain, we will see that the same thing is repeated in those countries with the difference that those countries also exhibit their own productions with the same thematic content that represents a grave danger even to adults, not to mention adolescents and children who become intoxicated and make themselves slaves of the cinema, and like drunkards become permanent victims.

One could argue that this type of film is usually prohibited to minors in the capitals or large cities. Meanwhile in the interior and provincial cities such things do not happen, since minors make up the greater number of movie-goers and furnish the largest source of income to the cinema. At times minors will steal from their parents, relatives and friends or even from anyone on the street to go to the movies.

The producers and proprietors of theatres do not care about the source of their income, once the money passes through the ticket-window, because it means little to them and they do not trouble themselves about this matter. Society is not interested in the reasons for a crime, if some individuals transgress the law and for this reason such an individual no longer belongs to society but lies under the jurisdiction of the law or in the hands of a psychiatrist or a doctor who will be his judges. They will then decide on the need to isolate the transgressor in an asylum or a prison or release him anew to society after making him pay a certain amount of money, depending on his personality and personal wealth.

The same process is repeated frequently. However, the same society forgets to take the necessary measures for the prevention of a crime and the fact is that if these precautions were taken, the crime would not be committed.

Let us turn again to the French movie, taking as an example *Le Diable au Corps* (Devil in the Flesh) which shows the sexual love of a woman. It mobilizes, in conjunction with Clouzot's *Manon*, the carnal splendor of a heroine whose first name served for a long time as a synonym for prostitution. The film *Assurance sur la Mort* (Pact with the Dead) combines an eloquent demonstration of a perverse crime with eroticism. Let us note that each of these films presents an excuse, an alibi, exacted by circumstances that are hypocritical, such as divine punishment in *Manon;* the heroine of *Diable au Corps* (Devil in the Flesh) and the assassin of *Assurance sur la Mort* are punished not by the law of man but by a divine one. Such is the cinema, at times excellent, frequently admirable, that is placed at the disposal of the people along profitable lines, planting seeds of delinquency and motives of crime.

None of the films that are shown on our screens is in general produced for youngsters with the exception of the efforts of Sonica Bó, director of the Club "Cendrillon" of Paris and a few other people, who followed his example disinterestedly. These cases are not numerous and it is truly difficult to consider them as a success that may solve the problems of children in the modern cinema. It is a serious problem, but always hoodwinked. Thus, the cinema does not think of children while the children think of it much too much and this makes us foresee and feel bad consequences.

Many see the danger but a kind of taboo makes a sort of silence imperative. This type of film is so detrimental that it should not be shown to the general public. Why not? Certainly that is better than to have systematic mental detractors. The system that tries to defend itself through censure is almost always wrong and has a sense that is contrary and is at times the source of evil that forms all the conventions of obscure morality.

Louis Bertrand of the French Academy, in his review *Pedagogie*, November 1949, stated: "I have no opinion about the cinema nor will I ever set foot in a motion-picture theatre." The man who said this is a cultured man who has written many books.

He most certainly is a very conservative man who has not progressed, because the cinema is a sign of progress that not only entertains but serves as a source of training and is a vehicle for a knowledge of culture in general and a consequence of the development of civilization. We cannot become enthused with this example that is followed by a quantity of others, who often claim they have common sense and often are very ignorant. Here is the opinion of a very "Parisian" paper "Le Combat," on the film *Manon* by Clouzot: "Here is a film where the principal interest lies in prostitution," says the journalist, 'vagrancy, desertion, barbaric crimes, murder of innocent people, and the most vile vocabulary in the French cinema . . . is it surmisable to ask then, what should be the characteristics of a film that receives such a denunciation interdiction. The vehemence of the journalist is not justified. I contend he exaggerates a great deal but newspapermen often do. They have to get headlines, and I myself, who work for the press, can understand this striving for the sensational. Often it is well to let people know the risks they run. For many viewers, and even Clouzot, the principal interest of the film is aesthetic and the Seventh Art, by criticizing certain customs, should really cause great interest. If we should interrogate these censors they will answer essentially that they cannot divulge the secret of the Council's deliberation—as though this were a professional secret—truly a hypocritical answer but we can understand their embarrassment; and the answers show their ignorance. Actually there is another reason based on commercial considerations. The French cinema and others, with the exception of the American, are suffering financial difficulties, and this is attributed to the producers. In Brazil, the admission prices are very low and movie theatre owners cannot rent films of artistic quality because most of the public cannot understand them. As the public is used to films with vulgar emotions and cheap sensations, the suppression of this type of film would scare away the usual public. The proprietors cannot afford to take that risk.

The censors' problem with *Manon* was whether or not they should authorize and permit women of ill repute to educate a large number of young girls or prohibit it to children. The censors would thus be harming a film that shows the most respectable artistic effort in our day and gives a true version of the literary work. The French Commission chose the first possibility for very special reasons that do not interest us in our study. The French Commission's problem is repeated daily throughout the world. Often officials are in a quandary about making a decision. When it is difficult to make a decision, they will hide under bureaucratic immunity and thus not commit themselves; in other cases bribes, political and social influence play an important part. This sometimes reaches such proportions that no oral or written protests can immediately remedy the situation; only a tightening of censorship laws and/or better educated audiences could gradually change this current condition.

For example, tuberculosis would not be conquered just by prohibiting coughing nor venereal diseases erased just by using palliatives. A newspaper in Haut-Marne in France published an article on what happened in a projection room the moment the film *La Maison du Maltais* is shown. The film was prohibited for those under 16 years of age, and this measure started a scandal. A gentleman, accompanied by his wife, faced this interdiction by taking his eighteen-month-old son with him. The guard, carrying out the law—"a law is a law"—asked them to leave the theatre. The public protested violently against the intervention of authority over the country. The occurrence frightened and scandalized the public but it is common to take children of this age to the cinema; the danger is great and all the doctors agree on this fact. It does not take a doctor to know that an eighteen-month-old boy must sleep at night in bed and not in the arms of his mother while she watches a film—in this case *La Maison du Maltais* (The House of Maltese).

In a western film, horse thieves are pursued by a group of ranchers while the following dialogue is heard "I'll show them, Bill, how we can get the Sheriff's son."

Another example, a spectator coughs a long rythmic cough, not from the grippe but from nervous emotion. A man intensely nervous, says something in the woman's ear. "Are you sure the child is asleep?" "I'm certain, he sleeps," she answers, "because I gave him the necessary dosage. Embrace me!" By saying this the woman meant that she had drugged the child in order to be able to go to the movies without giving up her sensual pleasure. This is a criminal truth, but the truth is that there are pharmacists who will oblige the drug purchaser under such circumstances. They may even provoke an act that really shows the ignorance of a bad mother. With this clear example, we cannot doubt that the cinema provokes delinquencies and even bloody crimes.

As another example of aggression, the dog on the screen continues to free the horse that is a prisoner of the robbers; then the horse frees its owner and the owner in turn is able to free the dog that had been apprehended anew. The lights go on. THE END.

An adolescent, leaving that world of make-believe and returning to the normal world; yells: "Did you see that bandit and how he 'got the other'?" This is slang, often the language used. And he jumped on the shoulders of his friend and hit him in the manner in which the screen villain in the movies got it from the cow-boys, and the friend, still groggy from the dark hall, takes a knife from his trousers and attacks his pal, just like he had seen it done in the movie a short while before. The sad result is a fellow being carried to a hospital, seriously hurt, and the other facing a judge, although this had to do with youngsters of only 14. All these details are actual and can be verified. This occurred in a city in the interior of France, in a town theatre.

Jean Chasel, Judge of Minors of the Department of Seine said the following:

"Of the twelve children we see in court a day, eight or nine go to the cinema four times a week; as a rule on Thursdays, Saturdays and Sunday afternoons and evenings. Three of the delinquent children had gone to the cinema 23 to 27 times within a month and were doubtlessly mentally disturbed. Whose fault is this? Evidently the cinema's and certainly, their environments.

Giving a lecture in 1950 in Algeria before a group of students, Dr. A. Piershe said the following:

"I had a patient, an adolescent of 16, whose attitudes left me nonplussed. He had no visible illness, he seemed well-balanced, intelligent but he hardly spoke at all and seemed little interested in the world around him. They had let him go from the job he had and he had not yet told his mother, a weak, sickly, alcoholic woman. It was said that he went to the cinema daily. In fact, had done so for two years. How can anyone go to the cinema seven times a week? 'Seven, nothing' the boy said, 'nine. Saturday twice and Sunday twice.' In this fellow's case he barely knew how to speak. Whose fault was it? The cinema's and the mother's who didn't know how to bring up her child. We ask ourselves: should women like this be allowed to have children? No law impedes it. But each case is an imposition on society, apart from the cinema's guilt."

This is what M. Poulain, Director of the Adolescent Reform School on Vaugirard Street in Paris said:

"A young boy of 12 left his home every Sunday at mid-day and only returned on the following morning. In accordance with his own words, during the lapse of this time, he would go to different motion pictures. To obtain the admission fee, he would beg in the subways.

We were surprised one day by an exchange of proposals

where one of our adolescents, an especially avid movie-goer, proposed to one of her friends to commit an act of prostitution to solve the question of money."

Still another example where the cinema and particularly the sequential image serve indirectly as instruments of crime. Mr. Rosie Maurel, delegate to the division supervising delinquent minors and attaché of the Ministry of Justice of Paris said in the *Journal Popular* of May 1951:

"In accordance with our records, there are many youngsters who go to the movies five and six times a week. Under these conditions they are obliged at times to have the images "drawn out of them" and often require hospitalization in a preventive-curative type of mental clinic or reformatory."

We must think in terms of the enormous consumption that the movies have, not only as far as money is concerned but in raw materials of infinitely greater importance, such as time or imagination. At present television and 3D divides activity with Lumiere's cinema. Ranking with the development of the oil industry, Americans are just as interested in developing the motion picture industry and many producers will devote time to glancing through world literature and folklore in quest of inspiration for future films.

A fellow after seeing a French film *Poil de Carotte* where an attempt at hanging is made, wanted to repeat the scene he had witnessed in the theatre. If the parents had not arrived at the crucial moment, in time to save their son who was trying to hang himself, he would have died.

Here we have not only an attempt at crime but the cinema presenting itself in the primary role of assassin. Consider a statement made by Dr. Wazenne, who was responsible for a clinic for social rehabilitation cases:

"One day a young boy imitating Tarzan, climbed a tree and wanted to jump; grabbed at and tried to swing from the branch of a tree and thus broke his arm in several places. He had seen an American film *Tarzan, The Ape Man*. This boy, a victim of the cinema, is now handicapped for the rest of his life."

Who should be reprimanded for this—the producer, the director of the theatre, or the cinema itself? Dr. Wazenne continues:

"I knew another case of a fellow who only wanted to imitate explorations of the heroes he admired on the screen. He jumped from the top of a large wardrobe, once attempting to strangle himself in the act. Here is another example of images that kill suddenly, although indirectly, but in the end there is another dead body.

A group of street urchins after seeing a wild West movie and a fight with Indians, when they left the cinema tied a friend to a tree and burnt his feet. To keep him from crying out, they put a kerchief over his mouth as they had seen done on the screen.

After this treatment on the part of his maniacal pals— who were imitating what they had seen on the screen, the poor fellow spent three weeks in the hospital with second-degree burns. We can cite hundreds of cases like this.

The cinema is obviously responsible, certainly with regard to adolescents. An excerpt taken from Dr. Juliette Boutonier's Book *Angoise*—she is the Director of Psychology of the Department of Pedagogy of the Paris Academy which I attended —reads:

"The cinema is more like a dream than art and it places the spectator in a state of passive receptivity, for which we can hardly find a comparable equivalent, at least up to now— since in dreams we are the authors as well as the spectators. On this aspect, the pleasure from the cinema is really like the most elemental of pleasures; those that appeal to pure receptivity—without reciprocation—for example, like the pleasure of drinking. It is not just a coincidence that the cinema and alcohol act as substitutes in certain instances."

In this area we see another aspect of the cinema where it

acts as an intoxicant and powerful narcotic in a way harmful as alcohol can be in heavy dosage or a small quantity of cocaine. Although we will combat the cocaine salesman, considering him a criminal, we do not regard the producer of a crime-inducing film as a delinquent. Why do we make this distinction, since the result is the same and the film creates so much perturbation?

Dr. Le Moal mentions the fact that Jean Gabin was not chosen as a favorite actor by the group of boys this psychiatrist examined, except in the case of delinquent children. To these youngsters Jean Gabin was identified with the type of role he usually played in the films such as *Pepe le Moko*, *Au delà des grilles* (The Walls of Malapaga) and later *Victor* adapted from Henri Bernstein's work and a "MAIC" production from the Neuilly-sur-Seine, Paris studios on which I collaborated—*Quai des Brumes* (Port of Shadows) etc.

According to the newspaper "Le Monde" in 1951 there were 400,000 mentally deficient children in France. To say that the cinema is culpable for this total would be ridiculous but in 25% of the cases it is guilty—not only in France but throughout the world wherever the cinema exists.

Here is an opinion of specialists in the subject:

"The super or hyper-emotional and obsessed are the ones who run the greatest risk in witnessing scenes of strong impact. Within the highly emotional child there is an innate tendency, almost pathological, to feel everything with extreme intensity; the obsessed are so impressionable that every experience of this type is a constant source of conflict within them.

At the exact moment of projection the hyper-emotional child experiences by watching the film the same physical and moral pains as the heroes. He fears for them, cries, tries to change their thoughts, covers his eyes in order to shut out the screen or closes his eyes; he will become agitated, bite his nails and will experience such physical manifestations as perspiring, tremors, the need to void, anguish, etc. And as in the case of the youngster who fell from the tree after he saw Tarzan and the other who tumbled from the high wardrobe, we see that the cinema distorts the realities of life; it is truly a threat in that it shows people who walk on live coals, fall into deep water without drowning, place themselves in the line of machine-gun fire without falling. In a superficial way, not only a dangerous example is suggested to the spectators but beyond that the impression is redoubled by a suggestion of possibilities even greater than in regular life. The cinema shows the act, the crime, and makes it seem very simple. Since there is no consciousness of the danger (the young mind is very susceptible) this is one of the worst results of the motion picture. What a shameful situation since if well-directed, the cinema could become a tonic for the young minds.

We can quote one of the outstanding post-revolution Russian directors—Eisenstein who said: "The cinema can say everything; it can exalt, or it can also destroy."

In 1950 statistics revealed that in 600 films shown in France without counting the serious offenses and crimes (those will be the subject of a separate study) there were 184 cases of perversion in the case of minors, 233 feminine and 275 masculine adulteries. Besides, the vague perturbation conscious or unconscious provoked by heated kisses, naked dancers or a strip-tease or can-can dance, bloody scenes, etc. should not be discounted.

Thus the cinema frees forces of which it is not cognizant; very often it is the long range effect that is dangerous. What is bad is not the cinema in itself, but this blind, unconscious orientation by delayed action bringing about mental explosives, the ultimate consequences of which are unlimited on the mind and unpredictable.

A sound, a photograph, optical vision, an obscene illustration, a radio or television show, a song, a newspaper article, can affect the psychological reactions of children—in fact, even of adults—bringing the moments of anguish. The moving picture that the cinema shows us is a palpable thing, the most powerful media for suggestion and the most widespread. Very often the adult and the adolescent can resist it, but the child almost never.

It should be observed that in the cinema the boss always marries the lovely secretary; the prince, the peasant girl. There we find a new mythology. Luck as in roulette, the lottery, the horse races, plays a disproportionate role. The heroes seem to live on air; the lumberjack never has to chop wood, the farmer only plows in a spot that is photogenic for the horse and the plow and when he truly plows as in the film *Farribique*, it seems that the public protests, under the impression that it is not realistic! The fugitive from justice lives in a sumptuous dwelling at Palm Beach, in California or on the "Côte d'Azur." Justice always triumphs in the end but the harm has been done. Very rarely on the screen are assassins undiscovered, bandits not placed behind bars, or robbers not captured. But why do we kid ourselves about this? There are thousands of crimes committed daily throughout the world and yet we speak only of those that are found out. In my opinion, these discovered crimes do not even represent 20% of all the offenses committed, after deducting all the crimes that are known but not publicized by reason of "pull" or influence with higher-ups. What a false picture the cinema can present to children and adolescents!

We will find the answers to all these riddles in the research study completed by Professor Heuyer, of the University of Paris, a doctor connected with the Children's Court in Paris. In his clinic for maladjusted children he had several cases of youngsters who had become disturbed due to the influence of the movies (See my book: *The Cinema and the Child* in which I mention some of Professor Heuyer's studies of different cases. I was present at some of his sessions).

Henri Michaud of the Ministry of Justice has said:

"A very moral film, if it develops in a prosperous setting, can frustrate many youngsters when they compare it to their own poverty-stricken surroundings. These effects can be more serious than those of *Quai de Brumes* (Port of Shadow) or *Hotel du Nord* (Hotel of the North) etc. where extreme wealth is shown. Henri Wallon, Professor of Psychology at the Sorbonne, adds:

"In a general way, we can say of the film that a child more than an adult is apt to identify a dream with a reality. A false universe, such as we present to them, threatens to mold their vision of the world most erroneously" (Notes and Documents).

In a film like *Bal de Sirenes* (The Siren's Ball) that is considered immoral by some, the danger is not that it may become an obsession with us but rather in the very insignificance of the film, its idiocy, its intellectual misery, its artifices, that hide the lavishness which it does not dare to show openly, so that both young and old spectators, once out of the fictitious world of the movies refuse to face reality.

The Magistrate Council in 1948 warned the French people to put a halt to this criminal influence of the cinema. The text follows:

"The abundance of gangster and detective movies, replete with technical details on the handling of a gun or preparation for attack, actually represent a school for crime that provokes in the young people and especially in the children, the psychological trauma of which similar traces are found in the trials of innumerable criminals."

On July 16, 1949 a decree-law was passed, regulating children's comics but the same could not be done for the cinema.

Juvenile delinquency and its connection with the cinema deserves a special and detailed study, completely objective but hard to realize, because the greatest number of those who express their opinions are more or less conscientious in the measure of their likes and their personal interest and they may be adversaries or defenders of this type of cinema. In Brazil, for example, juvenile delinquency is a strong factor and there are few good critics there although there are some who are apt to call themselves "official appointees" and their opinions may or may not be justifiable. Often their comments on the merits of the film tend to influence the otherwise informal opinion of the public.

The film personalities seem to bring the characters to life. The mechanism is very simple and quickly absorbed. In their playful ways, the young spectator imitates the gestures of their hero on the old game of cops and robbers, where the former always win.

The child goes along playfully with a wooden sword, a make-believe revolver, a good imitation machine-gun; from the cinema he learns that it is just as easy to pull the trigger of a revolver or of a machine-gun that shoots real bullets and may kill. It is a prologue to crime. This child will grow and it could be that the cinema image that has been well-kept within him for years will come into the open after the smallest conflict with his environment. If the image has been retained only dimly in his memory, he will find it strengthened by seeing a new gangster film where blood flows and the shots are multiplied; in this case bodies do fall and then there is prison. All of our arguments are insufficient to blame only the movies but may give reason to prove a portion of the guilt of crimes are provoked by the films. Evidently it is a factor. Really the movies are not the only factor to be held responsible but one must admit that there is a connection between child crimes (not to mention adult) and the cinema.

In the last 30 years children's crimes have noticeably increased in France. In 1935 the number of minors judged in court was 10,554 and in 1945 it was 23,384. The total fell a bit in 1948, but advanced again in 1953 to 32,000, an increase of 21,000 in relation to 1939, that is almost 300% and that

American film: GONE WITH THE WIND
Vivien Leigh and Clark Gable
Directed by Victor Fleming

American film: THE SNAKE PIT
Olivia de Havilland
Directed by Anatole Litvak

American film: ALL THE KING'S MEN
John Derek, Broderick Crawford, and John Ireland
Directed by Robert Rossen

British film: THE BROWNING VERSION
Michael Redgrave, Jean Kent, and Nigel Patrick

correlates directly with the increase in the number of theatres and the progress and development of the cinematographic industry.

Meanwhile in France in the last 30 years crimes of passion have hardly increased. There are always some 850 to 1,000 such crimes per year. After innumerable studies in France, England and the United States by the doctors, psychiatrists, lawyers, judges, professors and educators who made an effort to eliminate the influence of the cinema in the increase of delinquency, especially in the younger group, things remain the same and very little has been accomplished.

The International Institute of Filmology in Paris, together with the International Institute Against Crime, have tried to find a solution but they cannot solve the problem without the help of society, of motion picture producers and financial backers who ought to try to make films of higher quality, instead of money-makers with no artistic or cultural value.

A true threat to society is the trash in black and white or even in color or 3D in which all the damaging factors producing strong emotional reaction are shown in the film and are exploited by the dishonest producer. Here are some analyses of the different French tribunals:

A judge in the Children's Court in Rodez reported:

"A gang of boys from nine to thirteen who had been caught often in repeated robberies, explained their crimes by saying they had to have money to go to the movies. Wanting to go to the movies often contributes to delinquency."

Dr. P.......of Indre, France, of the Adolescents Court told about a boy of sixteen somewhat mentally retarded who earned his living by committing serious crimes in order that in his leisure time he might lead the kind of life he saw in the movies; for example, that he might invite his friends for drinks and good dinners with champagne, and so forth. The sad fact is that he stole in order to live the high life that he saw in the cinema.

A social assistant of the court in Moselle told us of the case of five children from bourgeois families who went to a casino one night to steal bottles of liquor. During the period of questioning, the children admitted that they went to the cinema daily.

Mr. Poulain, director of a penal colony tells us:

"The case you will hear is typical. A boy of 16 tried to steal a professor's brief case. He then explained that he had seen a movie where the robber had done the same thing." Mr. Poulain pointed out that this was a clear case where the cinema had wrongly influenced a child.

A psychiatrist handling adolescents said:

"I have found that young murderers, those between 17 and 18 years of age, go to the cinema regularly. The cinema for them is like alcohol for older people. The families realize the danger and try to keep them from it, but to no avail. A judge has stated:

"As soon as they are interrogated about their mistakes, the greater number of the guilty ones blame the crimes they saw; the harmful results. Thus eight days after he had seen a gangster film a boy of 16-1/2 years, although living nicely with his family, was found as he was being subjected to a beating. Another of the same age, whose feelings were perturbed by an erotic film, upon leaving the movie, went up to a woman and exposed himself.

Mr. Fernand Plas, a lawyer of the Court of Appeals in Paris said that innumerable times he had to defend delinquent minors, and was certain of an association between their acts and their numerous trips to the cinema. However, this in itself is not enough for an accusation. Men of science must express themselves.

We could list so many other similar cases where the cinema has provoked crimes but this would begin to border on the repetitious. The fact remains that crime is on the increase in France, not to speak of other countries, as for example, Brazil, where there is no death penalty or life sentence. A survey was made in France in 1948 on the topic "Does the Cinema take children to prison?" and it was brought out that as soon as the children are questioned in front of a judge they mention films they saw and claim they were just imitating what they had witnessed.

A priest from Bethune reported:

"Two delinquents killed an old lady living on Brussels Street in Lille and the investigators discovered that the murder had only taken place a short time before and that the criminals had just been to a movie where they had seen a similar type of crime. (Here is a perfect example of the malevolent effect of the cinema).

Now, to summarize the main thoughts outlined here, let me quote Mr. Henri Michaud, a high official in the French Ministry of Justice:

"According to our Survey Department, 20% of the minors before they were taken to prison went to the movies daily— at times more than once. At least 80% attended shows once a week. Mr. Poulain, who was quoted before, believes that if a child should see a very sensational film, it could provoke a criminal impulse that is dormant in the delinquent. We see vestiges every day of the connecting link between the cinema and crime.

Henri Wallon, professor at the Sorbonne says:

"In the cinema, the child sees constantly the enjoyment in killing. Notice how the films will show the ways of using a gun. Learned men like Rouvroy regard the entire cinema as a factor in progressive demoralization, while others believe that only certain films are guilty of this charge. I am of the latter opinion.

Certain psychiatrists affirm that the cinema not only promotes the growth of various complexes but also aids in the liberation of contingent impulses engendered by them. Actors in the cinema are able to perform criminal acts that the spectator unconsciously wants to commit. Samuel Lowry feels that the film *Men and his Fellowmen* furnishes the satisfaction of a substitute for aggressiveness like gangsterism in *Tarzan* or Western films. The sexual tendency is seen in strip-tease films, love scenes, pin-up girls, etc. All this tends to corrupt production in Hollywood in order to create a trend that is really "gangsterism in the movies" and is at the same time personal with a tendency to exploit the baser human emotions. I will enter into this subject again with regard to the Brazilian experience at a later date.

The American producers are trying to earn money in two ways by making the films enjoyable to both adults and children at the same time, but they ignore the psychological differences between the two groups. That is why they now make for television the types of "Westerns" previously made for movies supposedly for the young, from the works of such great authors as James Fenimore Cooper and Jack London, excellent adventure specialists, no doubt. There is a great effort in them to hold the interest of the adults in a general way, but there is also danger for the youthful audience, since saloons, semi-nude chorus girls, drunks, fires, etc. are shown.

This same ambiguity is found in films for children based on fables, produced usually in color. These are geared for success on the basis of dual appeal. Examples of this type are *The Thief of Bagdad, A Thousand and One Nights, Ali Baba and the Forty Thieves,* etc. True, these were basically entertainment films for children, but it was necessary to adapt the scenario for adults, and here we have the dissonance and danger created by the American cinema. Still, producers in other countries do the same thing.

I will now give you an excerpt from one of J. P. Mayers' books. He is the author of *The Sociology of the Film.* We quote his views on the films shown in one of the British Cinema Clubs for children:

"With the exception of one or two occasions, when good films such as *My Friend Flicka* were shown, it was believed proper to project old Western films, dated slapstick comedies, Shirley Temple films, or comedies that were released twelve to fifteen years ago. They were considered very good, probably because the rentals were so very reasonable. I saw even older pictures; some of the old Tarzan films showed animals killing human beings. During these showing many children were completely horrified."

In Russia and currently in Poland the films act as media for an ideological system; the cinema for adults and for children is simply another collective service like the radio, the press, or railways.

Russian production is particularly abundant in the category of animated cartoons, such as *The Cat and the Fox, The Hunchback House, The Three Bears*, etc. These cartoons are more in accord with the children's mentality than those produced in America, because the Russians reject the jazz rhythms and stress qualities in folklore, music and colors that are closer to those of nature than are those of the films produced in Hollywood. On the other hand, the themes are quite different since they are a vehicle for the transmission of Communist propaganda, with the Western nations always portrayed in an infamous light. Very often their films inspire hatred for the West, provoking strong psychological reactions in both adults and adolescents; the latter become morbidly prejudiced without recognizing the basis of the whole matter.

Well-presented lies are accepted by those who don't hear anything to the contrary. The Russians try, through the cinema, to instill orthodox politics but this does not eliminate the need to invent new myths regarding the heroism of the Red Army. (quoted from the *Cinema and Radio Magazine* of Rio de Janeiro, June 1954.)

The problem of children and the cinema has become increasingly serious. The films we see are not geared to children.

They often are a serious shock to their nervous system. The cinema is a very strong stimulus to some children, as their instinct to imitate shows us clearly. The cinema satisfies their need to dream and creates another world for them, more real than their own, and children often will hide within this make-believe world. Before the war, the German-National-Socialists produced short films for adolescents and when Hitler came to power with his "appeal for combat," Dr. Joseph Goebbels, Minister of Propaganda, employed the cinema as a powerful intoxicating drug directed toward the masses, as in the filming of the Fuehrer's speeches to the members of the party and in the filming of sadistic anti-Semitic themes, showing the Jews in an unfavorable light, much as the Russians do today. The Germans were presented as supermen, the English as usurpers, the Americans as plutocrats and assassins, the French as beggars, and the Poles as swindlers.

All this was done to develop deep and permanent hatred, with the object of getting the people mentally prepared for war. Through the press, the cinema and the Hitler Youth (a special organization), propaganda was disseminated to make the people forget that they lacked butter and other necessities. The Nazis first proceeded to exterminate the Jews, explaining that once this "abscess" was drained out, all would be well. The cinema served as an instigating force for this bestial crime. When the Jews were almost liquidated and the remnants were being herded into the extermination camps, the Nazis began to implement the same policy, always supported by the cinema, against Russian Communists, Poles and others who fought with the French, the English and the Americans.

Although we saw here an entire people mesmerized by the cinema, we cannot say that World War II erupted due to the movies. That would be an absurd assumption, but every absurdity has a kernal of truth and if we analyze the matter closely, we can arrive at a definite conclusion. One thing is certain; that the German cinema was instrumental in the extermination of the Jews.

The cinema was a contributing factor in the murder of several million Jewish people because it helped to hypnotize German morality. Once the whole question is thoroughly analyzed, the conclusion to be drawn is thoroughly shocking. The sad experiences with Hitler are now being repeated in Soviet Russia, where no one needs pay to see the cinema, where foreign film showings are very rare, almost non-existent. Only recently has there been some exchange of films then on a very limited scale.

Some films are obligatory for the Russian young people in particular, all those that depict the "heroism" of the Communist party. In fact, there are special showings for students where attendance is compulsory, and those who refuse to attend are seriously punished. We have a very good example of this in the case of an Italian film, *The Bicycle Thief*, which when shown in Moscow, had an insertion in the film of a speech by Palmiro Togliatti, leader of the Communist party in Italy. Obviously this degraded the film, since it was turned into an instrument for political exploitation. Many times Russian propagandists will permit a whole series of Tarzan films to be shown, but giving the impression that the films were captured from the enemy in Berlin, when the Russian troops victoriously entered the city. An American newspaperman who saw these Tarzan films, remembered having seen them fifteen years before. However, at the time when Russians showed these films, they asserted that these were the best recently produced American films, claiming that the Russian censor would not stand in the way of free expression in the cinema and were always making every effort to show the best bourgeois films, when they were worthwhile and could be put freely into circulation.

It was said in Moscow that during the winter of 1953, the Tarzan films caused quite a stir of comment in the Soviet

Union regarding American bourgeois circles. Before the films were projected, there was always a fantastic "documentary" commentary depicting the difficulties and struggle involved in getting these American films. This was described in detail by E. Emanuelli, one of the correspondents of *Bianco e Nero* (White and Black), an Italian magazine.

The only common denominator of the American and Russian censorship was in the case of the Italian film *The Bicycle Thief,*—the scenes deleted both in the U.S. and U.S.S.R. were those in which a little boy has to attend to his needs in the park. Both Russian and American censors were scandalized. In France and Italy, on the contrary, that scene was accepted as perfectly normal and very human.

Without a doubt there is reason to conclude that the Soviet cinema in recent years is not up to the standard set by Russia in those films produced after the first World War. What was best in the Soviet cinema in the years 1926-1940 was uninhibited dramatic action, and today's productions seem to have lost that quality. Turning from the revolutionary lyricism to didactism, the Soviet art was deprived of the essential creative element; its soul was crippled in the same manner as the Russian spirit.

Going from the dynamic myth to mechanized propaganda, the Soviet cinema seriously showed its inferiority by falsifying the spirit of the population by reactionary trends and artificial ones that give a dangerous impression of civilization on the other side of the Iron Curtain. All this provokes hate—as only the cinema can. Through its media it can really become very powerful, as powerful as a bomb. In fact, the damage made by a bomb may eventually be forgotten, but the seed sown by a movie lasts for years, and can be revived easily. Often this harm is not even direct but does react indirectly on the population of a nation. From an artistic point of view neither *A Real Man* nor *A Young Guard* by Guerasimov found the link with older works, as have today's classic films like *Potemkin,*

Arsenal, The Earth, Mother, etc. Certainly the films were dictated by a will that was methodical in communicating to spectators truth, according to the Soviets. Although they benefited from the great genius of some men, they followed their official control in every way, to correspond to a different spirit, the love of one's neighbors, the feeling of fraternity, showing a truly sublime spirit of soul as is seen in the film *Mother* that is also repeated in *Potemkin*, almost a representation of a community and an act of love.

This is seen in Vera Baranowska's scene at the end of the film *Mother* where there is such sublime greatness that one seems to be catapulted from one's seat. We are indebted to Russia for the following great films *The Fragment of an Empire, Village of Sin, Matriculation 12* etc. The Soviet cinema was able to touch some of the summits of emotions. There is always deep sorrow, and the martyrdom of a people shines forth. Only the great masters like Eisenstein (who died in Russia) and Poudovkine can communicate in this subtle manner the lyrical intuition and the universal impulses of this perturbed collective mass that is the Soviet Union today. The epoch becomes more and more turbulent. The Russian cinema, like all the others, triumphs by its magic over the habitual obstacles that impede us from seeing things clearly, because they see them every day.

The cinema makes us aware of how other peoples live. That is a great danger because the cinema teaches us that this universe is a world where misery, evil and horror exist in an never-ending chain. This is the funereal parade of humanity. I do not agree with Henri Angel, in his collection *Seventh Art* when he says that only puerile souls revolt at sadness.

In some films all generous men will, on the contrary, admire a medium that can integrate and expand visually on matters that they knew only along abstract lines. As you see, Mr. Angel, the problem is not as simple as you think, because one is hemmed in by life.

Man always rejects the truth about life, even if it is powerful. The misery that touches him from nearby does not produce a reaction in him, does not even seem real to him, whereas in the cinema, it is different. The producer and the cameraman are responsible for presenting an image in such a plastic manner that the viewer cannot forget it, and that is where the danger begins. The spectator feels the impact of the cinema and in a highly emotional state reflects on the difference from his own life and wonders how his problems can in turn be solved.

There are people who begin to believe in the artificial life of the cinema and accept it as a final reality, and this brings sorrow and complications of all kinds. This is specially true when in our society we have abnormal people who are partially or permanently disturbed and often suffer from psychoses such as sadism and superiority complexes. There are under-developed children, mentally retarded ones, some with sexual maladjustment, as well as impotence of both sexes.

The great emotions that the cinema can evoke may have on these groups the most deplorable consequences in the world, resulting in violence and murder. Evidently, it is difficult to know immediately whether the man who goes to the cinema has a mental illness or not, or whether he is merely a nervous individual. It is impossible to separate and control this type of cinema-goer, nor can one prevent such people from viewing scenes of exaggerated sexual moments, of bloodshed, temptation, death or other scenes that may induce an excessive accumulation of strong emotions. The only way to impede such viewing is not to produce films of this type. However, the profits in production would then diminish, since the great number of people cannot understand films that do not have strong emotions. The producer would have to make numerous films without being concerned about the value of art for art's sake.

The cinema would lose its power and it would be reduced

to a secondary level as an entertainment factor of no importance thereby becoming a vicious circle; only the viewer can choose. I will now give you still another example of what the cinema means and how powerful its psychology is—it is taken from an Italian paper in Terracina, a town near Rome,—a motion-picture house showed a film on San Francisco's earthquake. A piece of plaster was falling from the ceiling and the spectators panicked and ran toward the exit: There were three dead and twenty wounded. In 1939 during the war, an English movie director saw an American film *Destry Rides Again*. It was the night that London's Trafalgar Square was hit by bombs. They fell all around Piccadily. The theatre was full and he never witnessed such applause for what was going on in the screen. But the audience took it in stride and was completely engrossed in what was going on in a bar in the "Far West." Every time James Stewart fired his revolver there was warm applause. We see here an example of the collective hypnosis of the cinema, where even a bomb could not shake the people loose from their artificial universe full of synthetic adventure that the cinema presented, reducing them to a state of trauma and temporary lethargy—giving them a little relief—while the true psychological reality outside went unnoticed. Counselor-at-law Campinchi of France has said:

"It is always harmful for a man to be forced to carry out a strict regulation. In fact, for some children, the movies have the effect of *Peyotill*, that Indian product that makes the eyes cloudy. Crime movies do that for children today—it is their Peyotill."

Professor Wallon is of the opinion that cinema for youth can be adequate, not only to diminish the current bad features of the motion picture, but also to utilize the virtues of that medium. There are those who say that the actions on the screen can mold the conscience of the child. It is very poetic to say this, but such phrases are meaningless. Culpable also are the parents who take children to the theatre or advise

them to see films which are not on a level with their mentality
and which cannot be accepted by a child. We can repeat
what Alexandre Arnoux of the Concourt Academy has said:
"There are two kinds of men. The old and the young—
and the cinema separates them. The old come first, the young
second. Our men of politics are in the first group. They truly
understand the industry of the cinema but not its moral importance. They see enough films and they have time, but
they are slow to understand." (From Muet au Parlant, La
Nouvelle-Edition, 1946). The date given below reflects the
opinion of Prof. Henri Wallon, a specialist in Children's
Psychology of the French College, and one of the greatest
authorities in the country, with regard to the cinema psychology and the relationships between those two sciences.
These conclusions are so interesting that we will cite several
passages: It is possible in certain ways that the cinema may
be one of the factors that bring children to juvenile court.
But how to determine the importance of this factor in relation to other factors! To make a categorical statement on
this seems to me premature. However, without a doubt the
cinema does influence the behavior of children. In a general
way, we can say that before a motion-picture screen, a child,
more than an adult, tends to identify himself with a dream,
with a falsified universe, that becomes his vision of the world.
It also places him in a position or situation that his mind
cannot comprehend. The very young child will also live
in the dream world of the movies.

The incoherent reaction patterns that are produced by
certain themes and also the violence witnessed may definitely
influence the psychological development of the child.

In gangster films, I feel that it is not the hero but the
proper plastic force and the cinematic film expression that
holds the child's attention. In the cinema, the child constantly
sees the enjoyment of killing. He is shown how to handle
a revolver and cause death. These acts are executed with

great facility, and the aesthetic vitality of these scenes is clearly imprinted on their mind. Will he tend to imitate that which he saw on the screen? Will his conscience escape the restraining qualities of morality? The different cases that we read about in the newspapers speak of lamentable homicides. A predominant and grave question for all the countries that have cinema arises: to diminish the bad features of the cinema and at the same time utilize the virtues of this media. In France, there are approximately 4,150 movie theatres that are patronized each week by almost five million theatre-goers —among them a million and a half children. We will mention some of the opinions of professionals who are in regular contact with children. In a study made by a French magazine *L'Ecran Francais* (The French Screen) in 1938. The cinema may be a great art form and a valuable means of education; however, what does it provide at present for these children? Films that are made by and for adults, films that exalt the brutal force of crime. In the 400 films shown in France in this year there were 310 death, 120 robberies, 320 cases of adultery, masculine and feminine, etc., and in 9 cases out of 10 the films are mediocre. That is the opinion of authorities on the subject.

The opinion of a doctor:

It is not necessary to sacrifice the beauty of a walk or the joy in listening to a child's conversation. Most of the films, even the best, show scenes of terror that have a profound influence on children's spirits.

The opinion of a teacher:

The principal defect in the students is their lack of concentration. This is increased by the movies on the screen where they will see everything quickly and superficially. Children viewing a film for adults cannot understand it all. Their ideas are confused and their spiritual development is warped. Many films present an unreal world to children.

A children's judge:

The number of young delinquents brought to court is constantly increasing. The cinema is not the only cause of this, but it certainly contributes to it, by showing numerous examples of immorality.

Now we will refer to the influence of the cinema on delinquency in general, the motives and the causes, and the measures that must be taken to abate it.

B. MOVIES: AN INTEGRAL PART OF SOCIETY

In the entire world each year some 15 billion 600 million people go to the cinema or over five times per man, woman, and child. Among them are some whom luck may turn into movie stars. On television one sees at present the same phenomenon. The real danger is found in rehearsing and remembering the misery of our daily lives on the screen. It is the film and not cinematic art that discredits true cinema, which is the Seventh Art. The friend of the Seventh Art penetrates into an imaginative universe in the cinema. The films transport him there through filming cameras into a strange cinematographic world.

In some cases the indivdual enters a different realm where the reality of the present is turned into imaginative hallucination. On the screen we see what the eye can see and we wonder whether it be a living personage from Mars, an abstract painting or a circulatory system of a frog. Like mushrooms on the land, the creatures of the imaginary world are fighting and devouring each other and thus there is war, and criminals, and assassins. The cinema is a kaleidoscopic picture of a section of our daily life that exploits sensation and emotion for commercial reasons. This is the principal danger for the audience.

This powerful eye can see a magic objective; horizons in obscurity which are directed along definite lines in which the spectator takes part. In life we die, we strive, we hate, we love—we are happy or miserable—all depends on good luck, on power, on education, character and health, and in fact all this may be reproduced by a good photographer.

The harmful effect on the audience—this is another problem—but for this reason alone, the producer will not be preoccupied. Only afterwards, the doctor, the educator and the judge will have the work of curing the individuals intoxicated by the cinema. This will make a sickly person out of a healthy one and a chronic patient out of a sickly one. We have before us different cases of mental abnormality, some induced by the movies and others made more severe by the movies. I do take great care in even suggesting that a large number of abnormal individuals are victims of the cinema. We also have hereditary and many other influences, and I cannot go into detail regarding this, but the cinema does have its place among them—and it is a serious place. The criminal power of the cinema is extended over television, cinemascope, 3D, cinerama, etc. Everyday life changes with such rapidity that we do not have time to realize what is happening. Each indivdual lives within his generation, he obeys the laws and lives within those laws. Man changes his point of view frequently. The motion picture producers try to give a picture more perfect than reality.

Frequently, the magic eye of a camera is more perfect than that of a human. We should take advantage of the marvelous power of the cinema, its perfection and its mystic power over the spectator, that very often provokes intoxication in the individual. The projectionist must project a great space of time in a few minutes, making it similar to a real life span. In many cases, moments of great climax are superimposed on the screen, that will exercise a bad influence on the young spectator. There are films that remind them of their own life or in certain instances, make them meditate on the bad and good in their own lives.

In the case in which the individual sees on the screen a
film that reminds him of his own life, he vibrates internally.
However, his external reaction may be eliminated in some
ways. Evidently a producer cannot know what is going on
in the inner self of the viewer, and this guilt is indirect in
the cinema, but the result is always the same. The fans of the
cinema may be satisfied that the screen does not kill indirectly,
the simple spectator will be satisfied with the fact that the
cinema is culpable. The enemies of the cinema and some con-
servatives will shout "Eliminate the cinema—the source of
all the crimes. Let us destroy the cinema, and delinquency
will diminish. In our time we did not have movies and we
were happy."

Each one of the witnesses comes to the same result, and
the answer is always the same, the witness accuses the cinema
of crime, but fails to offer a plan or a solution to abolish the
bad influences of the cinema. Further on in this book I will
try to suggest an intermediate solution that will not solve
the problem completely but will certainly assuage the evil.

The most developed areas of activity of the cinema are
the documentaries that appeal to the true strength of the
cinema and criticize social conditions. The problem of the
city, the farm, the nation, is presented with all its original force
on the screen. At present we can appreciate this situation
through the cinema, and witness all the problems of the whites
and negroes in America, their conflicts and differences; the
bloody battles between the whites and the redskins, who
today face extermination as a race.

The situation of the immigrants and those without a
country, the consequences of war, are depicted. The life of
the Japanese fishermen in "*Aci Trezza*" the inter-breeding of
the yellow race and its consequences in Asia. The life of
the explorer, his conquests and his suffering, scientific life, all
this represents the field of activity of the cinema which can
be explored either for good or bad purposes.

Jean Painlevé, the ex-president of the International Scientific Cinema, who was a delegate from France to the First Festival of São Paulo, Brazil in 1954, gave several lectures in the Hall of the Ministry of Education in Rio de Janeiro, the former capital, in which he showed different scientific films. Aims and values were pointed out. Here is a statement of his: "In the laboratory and in the school, the cinema is developed at an accelerated pace throughout the world. Academic science tries to use the cinema, even though it is not obligatory in teaching. But the form is useful in any case and the use of the cinema in education will not fail to make itself known and to reaffirm its utility. There are still many difficulties to be solved along practical lines, due to the high cost of the film and of experimentation with it, as well as along psychological lines, because the cinema has always been looked upon as an entertainment media. Most believe that the cinema is not a very serious thing. They consider it the same as an accomplice of a "Magic Lantern" which was once used as a means of education.

There is today a great movement in the whole world to have a closer collaboration between the organs that teach and the cinema, and between the cinema and culture. This tendency is directed by John Grierson and Jean Painléve, who constitute the vanguard of educational cinema.

The fields of education and cultural art started a battle against the common cinema and should come out as the winner, if people of good will help them.

II IS THE CINEMA
AN INCITEMENT TO CRIME?

Chapter 2

IS THE CINEMA
AN INCITEMENT TO CRIME?

Let us take a criminal case in which, contrary to all the cases already mentioned, the influence of the cinema is decisive, as a crime of double death. This case was divulged in 1913 by Guilherme Apolinaire in *Soirées of Paris* (Nights of Paris) at the beginning of continued cinematographic projection. We now verify that the cinema grew up in a tide of blood; therefore we must not doubt any more its influence on crime. We do not guarantee the historic authenticity of the fact, but we saw too many episodes of Mussolini's Fascism, Hitler's Nazism and we have therefore, no reason at all to doubt that, even more so when it was published as an historic and scientific fact by "The Harvill Press," in its issue of September 1950, in the magazine *Sight and Sound* reproduced by a French magazine *Le Positif* of Lyons, and reproduced anew by the Italian magazine *Bianco e Nero* 1953.

It is possible that this will be a cause of satisfaction for the authorities on the matter. I am not an authority, nor can I affirm or deny that the cinema is an instrument of crime, directly with the same force as a machine-gun, a revolver or a bayonet, or anything that may provoke death.

This case pertains to a movie considered to be a great film, without any technical magic or artifice, a real crime that must have greatly impressed its admirers and those who saw it on the screen without realizing that they saw a true story, called by the police "the perfect crime." It is a common crime, with many spectators, involuntary witnesses, where the true culprits were not found and innocent victims "took the

43

rap" which satisfied the police and "justice" triumphed. The
true culprits go on committing crimes. They did not call it
a judicial error in need of rectification. Very often eyes are
closed if the proof is not one hundred percent there, because
if justice makes any mistakes this is most damaging to the
nation which will not have confidence in it.

"Who can affirm that I have no crime on my conscience,"
Apolinaire has said, going on to state "with some friends we
had been able to create the International Cinematographic
Company and we wanted to produce interesting films to
distribute them in the principal capitals of Europe and America.
Our program was well organized. Thanks to the indiscretion of
a butler, we were able to obtain reproduction of the birth of
the prince of Albania (son of Prince William of Wied).
Greater success was the fact that we were able to film with
the aid of the Sultan's functionaries a tragedy in which the
Grand Vizier Melack Pasha says goodbye to his family and
drinks poisoned coffee right on the terrace of his own house
in Pera carrying out the order of his supreme patron and
owner, the Sultan. Our reel lacked a crime scene. As we could
not legally obtain one, we rented a villa in Auteil in Paris
and tried to film it using our own resources. We did not want
to exhibit forced scenes. Our custom was to present the truth.
We imagined filming a true homicide case but no one wanted
to partake in it. One night we hid with our revolvers near
the villa we had rented; there were about six of us, all armed
to the teeth; suddenly a couple went by, a man and a woman,
both young, and we thought they would do for our crime.
Threatening them with a gun, we bound them and took
them to our villa.

"We quickly returned to the place where we had captured
them and kidnapped an old man in evening clothes, in spite
of his resistance. When he saw the revolver, he decided to
accept his fate. Meanwhile, our operator had prepared everything in order to film the crime scene. We were on the side of

the operator, keeping our prisoners under gun threat; the two young ones had fainted. We undressed them carefully, leaving a flimsy under garment on the woman and only a shirt on the man. Then I turned toward our third prisoner, a gray-haired man, and told him that we did not want to harm him but that in exchange for his life, we wanted him to kill the couple, with the knife we had placed at his feet and thus furnish us with a crime scene that we needed to finish a film. Our future assassin answered: "One cannot argue against force; the decision is yours; I will not try to dissuade you; in order to protect myself, let me use a mask."

We allowed him this request and gave him a black kerchief with the holes for the eyes which he placed over his face and started the macabre sequence. He untied the hand of the young man and our operator started to film the fight scene: an armed person against an undefended one; a true slaughter scene. The assassin with the knife touches the arm of the victim. The young man, with the force that comes from terror, threw himself on the aggressor. It was a quick fight, but the woman rose to help her friend and fell with a stab in the heart. Immediately, our assassin returned to the man and after a short battle, cut his neck. The assassin was successful, the kerchief did not fall during the fight and then he asked us if we were satisfied. He washed his hands and asked if his mission were finished. At this point our camera stopped cranking. We congratulated him for the good work; we now had the principal scene. The assassin thought that we should hide the vestiges of our presence because certainly the police would be going to the site next day. We left together; the assassin said goodbye like a "gentleman" and each one went on his way. It is obvious that we were not going to bed after such an adventure. The next day the newspapers spoke of the crime; it had to do with the wife of a diplomat and her lover; they were the victims. We had rented the villa under an assumed name: the agent was not able to identify the victims to connect them with us.

For many months the police followed the wrong scent. The newspapers explored the fact in big headlines, speaking of the incapacity of the police in solving the mystery. You can imagine the success that we had upon projecting such a film with an advertisement that had to do with a true crime. The Police gave no credence to the incident—they thought it was a bit of publicity on our part. The public too did not disappoint us.

After six months of showing the film throughout Europe and America each of the members of our company received 342,000 francs. That was a fabulous sum in those days. The crime caused so much notice that the police arrested a suspect of another crime and in spite of his protests of innocence, as he could not give an alibi for the night of the crime, he was condemned to death."

Everyone tried to create the impression, including the press and the public, that the police are ever vigilant and that justice never sleeps and repeat the old "slogan" *crime does not pay*. Furthermore, we were very satisfied once the case was closed and the victim executed. Our cameraman arranged to be present during the execution and filmed the last moments of the condemned victim. After, we showed this particular film to the public stressing always a natural image, without subterfuge. Within two years we made a million francs and separated by liquidating the company." Thus Apolinaire terminates his macabre story adding: 'I lost my profits a year later, betting on the horses."

We may or may not believe this story; each can think as he likes but for my part I see no reason to doubt it; we have many such examples of crimes and of miscarriages of justice where the actual criminal is at liberty and was not punished and an innocent man paid for his crime with his life. I will not analyze this type of case separately with regard to the nature of the crime, or from the point of view of the penal or criminal rights. There are mitigating circumstances and if one segment of a story is true it will demonstrate sufficiently the criminal origin of the cinema and one cannot thus over-estimate its criminal influence either indirectly or at times, directly. Let us say that the members of that company were crazy, sadistic or perverse, but it did happen in the midst of our society and one does find such crazy people. We must not give them bad examples nor excite them through the cinema; on the contrary, we must do everything possible to put in practice preventive measures against them; in America alone, recent statistics show, more then 35 percent of the people are not normal—this without considering the world, as a whole. The only way to solve this is to revise the crime films and all those that provoke strong emotions; three-reel type films are not only dangerous for children and adolescents but also frequently for adults who are difficult to re-educate. Prison is not an adequate solution and its effect is at times harmful rather than helpful. It is easier to prohibit the production of films of this kind through international laws, severely punishing the transgressor and employing all of our efforts to make documentaries based on nature, in accordance with the needs of science and education.

Let me quote a poem by Guilherme Apolinaire entitled *Before the Cinema*

> "If we were artists,
> We would not say—the Cinema!
> We would say: The cine—
> But if we were old provincial masters
> We would neither say Cine nor Cinema
> We would say Cinematography
> Thus, by Heaven, we should have artistic taste."*

We will ask how can the cinema—the "Seventh Art" be regarded as an art when the greater part of its production is

*The stress of "artistic taste" by Apolinaire we have already seen.

devoted to sensational films that have no art at all. Our "sarcastic" Apolinaire, poet and writer, said that the film to be a true cinema should be based on art. Nero, in ancient Rome burns the city to satisfy his artistic taste. Hitler massacred innocents to establish a pure race of superior men, all this to satisfy the beauty of the arts. He killed thousands of Jews and Bohemians, cremating women and children. He did all this for the love of Art. Let us do away with this excuse that has been used too often. It only brings greater sorrow and pain. Let the example pointed out be clear and forceful for those who try to produce "gangster" films, saying that they do so for the love of art. And our hope is that there are not too many such "artists" in society interested in continuing the "artistic sadism" of Guilherme Apolinaire.

III ADOLESCENT CASE HISTORIES

Chapter 3

ADOLESCENT CASE HISTORIES

SPYROS SKOURAS, the motion picture magnate of Twentieth Century Fox, declared not so long ago that, thanks to the innovation of cinemascope (developed from Professor Chretien's invention) he is of the opinion that motion pictures have reached and perhaps surpassed the level attained by the theatre. Twenty years ago the great theatrical figure Max Reinhardt, while watching the Russian film *Potemkin,* said the same thing: "the theatre would give way to the cinema." It is possible. There are, however, few cases in which the theatre was responsible even indirectly for criminal actions. We do not doubt that the cinema can attain such perfection, whether it be in the form of Cinemascope or Cinerama, or under any other name, if it is that theatre art may ever be substituted for any cinematographic art, even united to television, in the future. Meanwhile, we should abolish everything that is not art in the cinema. Speaking plainly, we would exclude everything which I have called 'cine" in my study, as distinguished from true theatre art which should be the basis of the cinema. Everyone would profit by this procedure, especially the immature.

In society we find maladjusted people, psycopaths, weak individuals, and perverse ones. I will discuss some of these in the adolescent groupings.

If we look at the latest statistics on mental levels of the world's population, we will be greatly surprised because we will see that 25% of the total consists of mentally unbalanced individuals: 15% schizophrenics, 10% mentally retarded 5% of the latter being completely uncontrollable, lacking in moral strength and the ability to contain their impulses. However one cannot condemn the cinema even though it might be a minor factor in the abnormal condition that the cinema may develop in some human beings.

Let us consider certain cases in those infantile groups. Let us start with a maladjusted one, a dark boy from Martinique, named Ludovic. He is timid and kind, sad and easily frightened. He is conscientious in his work and even though he is not intelligent, he is very studious. Ludovic is nostalgic for the land where he was born and where he spent his first years, and was put into service by his own father. This primitive little fellow, forced to live within the four walls of a musty house in a poor section of Paris, went mad and broke everything. He also stole everything that he could lay his hands on. When remorse overcame him he ran away and disappeared for some days. He then returned home, like a dog with his tail between his legs, but planning to get away on a boat that could take him far away. He is not, however, sufficiently intelligent and energetic to carry out such an audacious plan. Very often his submission gives way to dissimulated revolt and brutality. His patience seems gone. Just hearing another person speak, maddens him and he hurts those who are trying to help him. He will crack the skull of a comrade by throwing stones. The rough words, the obscene songs that he learned reluctant to accept any educational aid. What can one do to help this poor fellow who will obey nothing but his instincts and will not yield to anything but force that makes him even more bestial! Probably this nature that has been frustrated will not re-adapt easily to the rural rife from whence it sprang. Like thousands of his countrymen, he will go and augment the proletarian rank and file and he will not absorb or assimilate anything but the vices of our "civilization." If we are on the loose, detective films, bloody pictures and all the other kinds that accumulate artificial sensations and strong emotions, this will only make the situation worse and we will have maladjusted and delinquent people, some of whom will become assassins, because in their morbid and uncontrolled mentality they will attempt to put into practice what they saw on the screen, using the same models and examples that the cinema offers. The above example or resume was taken from a study compiled by the Department for the Observation of Delinquents in Paris.

Another case was obtained from the clinic in Marseilles; this has to do with a psychopath called Simone. She is 13 years old, but has the appearance of 15. She wears heavy make-up and has exaggerated plucked eye-brows. Her father tells us that she goes out a lot with boys. Simone was sent to a special home and from there they had to take still greater care of her because of an hallucination that she had gone to an abandoned villa where a satyr had molested her and then tried to kill her. Her story was investigated and found to be absolutely false. Some time later Simone went to a dance with a boy of 16 and allowed herself to be taken to a dubious type of hotel where she remained for eight days. Simone pretended to have forgotten what happened—put on an amnesia act and then ran away with her drunken mother. Several days later she was found with her mother, both completely intoxicated. Simone was taken to a medical psychiatrist who discovered a deplorable hereditary trait on the mother's side. It was learned that one of her cousins had died from dementia and that an uncle too was insane. Simone had a long line of hereditary abnormalities.

In infancy, she had had every sickness imaginable. Her intelligence and her cultural assets in school seemed normal but she showed instinctive perversions: escapism and sexual promiscuity. She often complained of head-aches, of dizzy spells, of her hands shaking. When we placed Simone in a convent she tried to run away from the third floor of the dormitory with the aid of sheets. She fell on the pavement and fractured her skull. There was concern about her developing meningitis. However, she again ran away and left a note that read as follows:

"It is useless to try to find me. I'm going to drown myself."

After this attempt, Simone ran away again and turned openly to prostitution; this time she was committed to a home for wayward girls. However she could never adjust to the regimentation of a reformatory and, as escape was very difficult, she suggested to her friend that they set fire to the place, in the hope that they might escape during the commotion that the fire would cause. This suggestion brought about her transfer to Fresnes prison where she was given a comprehensive mental examination. The examination could not be completed since she was so irresponsible and society could no longer save this girl. It had to keep her from further harm to herself and she was committed to a mental institution in Marseilles for life.

Cases like that of Simone are encountered every day and if we allow young women like her to go to sadistic films and those concentrating on sexual themes, we will be responsible for these future delinquents as well as for girls of the street and hardened prostitutes.

We have another example that came to us from a rehabilitation colony maintained by the penitentiary adminstration in France. This has to do with a case of delinquency of a young fellow, George, and this is his story: At 12 he ran away from home, remaining away for fifteen days and stealing 4,000 francs. George has normal intelligence but is extremely slothful. He devoted so much time to masturbation that he was extremely weakened. At a very young age, George would take small objects from his home and school.

One day he was surprised by his teacher just as he was about to steal 600 francs from the director of the establishment. He fled on a stolen bicycle that was found abandoned later, not very far from the school. The young fellow headed toward Paris and arrived at the hotel where his father was

British film: PASSPORT TO PIMLICO
Stanley Holloway

British film: MURDER WITHOUT CRIME
Dennis Price

Italian film: THE PATH TO HOPE *(Il Cammino da Speranza)*
Raf Vallone and Elena Varzi
Directed by Pietro Germi

Italian film: THE BICYCLE THIEF *(Ladri di Biciclette)*
Lamberto Maggiorani
Directed by Vittoria De Sica

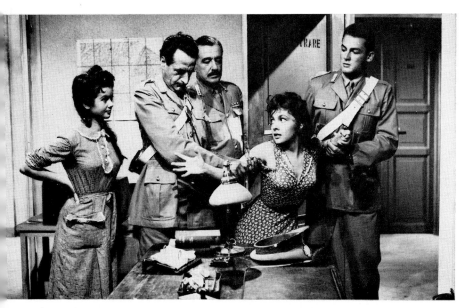

Italian film: BREAD, LOVE AND DREAMS (*Pan, Amore e Fantazia*)
Marissa Merlini and Gina Lollobrigida
Directed by Vittoria De Sica

Italian film: LA DOLCE VITA
Nadia Gray
Directed by Federico Fellini

French film: JUSTICE IS DONE *(Justice Est Faite)*
Claude Nollier
Directed by André Cayatte

French film: WE ARE ALL MURDERERS *(Nous sommes Tous de Assassins*
Raymond Pellegrin and Marcel Mouloudji
Directed by André Cayette

accustomed to stay, telling a false story to the hotel man. After remaining there a few days he departed, leaving a debt of 7,150 francs. He tried to get food in the establishment that supplied his grandmother. During his mother's absence, he entered his house through the window, broke open the cupboard and stole more than 3,000 francs. He took some clothing, choosing his best suit, purchased a suitcase and golf clubs and took off in the direction of Deauville, where he stayed in a hotel for several days under a false name.

He told the hotel man a fantastic tale, saying that his parents had sent him there for part of the summer in order to show how pleased they had been with his good marks and deportment in school. Somewhat intrigued, the hotel man ended up by calling the police and the boy was sent to a religious institution. On the very first night George ran away with another youngster, after stealing 500 francs from the priest who had been keeping an eye on them. At midnight when the police caught up with them, George said he was going to his aunt's house. That night he actually had gone to the house of his aunt, who had not been able to shelter him. Then he went to his grandparents house. After the first two days he had a pre-arranged plan regarding his future movements. He stole 3,000 francs and a watch and bought a bicycle with the money. He abandoned the bicycle soon after and started off in the direction of Cannes. Once there he spent eight days on the beach. Not having any more money, he took refuge in the house of another aunt. At his parents' insistence, the case was taken to Minor's Court, and it was learned that George had been seen in the company of a twenty-year old man of dubious character. A fire had started in a forest where they spent the night and both were accused of having started the fire.

Apprehended, George confessed everything, having spent all the money he had stolen. He pretended to have lost the watch which had actually been sold. He cold-bloodedly admitted his crimes without an iota of repentance. After this, he was committed for a time to a reformatory. This is an observation made regarding him during this period:

"He is too well-developed for his age. He has good eyes, a pleasant appearance, and he is well-groomed, which distinguishes him from the poor boys with whom he associates. He does not seem conscious of what it means to have lost his liberty. He will compare himself with his friends and consider himself more attractive than they are. He will dress and comb his hair in a peculiar way, trying to call attention to his type. He will brag about his robberies and his escapades with such daring that all wonder whether he is a cynic or simply unconscious of what he has done. He cannot resist his impulses or the requests of others, particularly if they have to do with satisfying a weakness to which he himself may readily be inclined. He is selfish and materialistic by nature. He adores living in an atmosphere of ease where no effort has to be made, and where he doesn't have to display his better qualities, nor obey anyone's orders. His escapades are nothing but the projection of his desires to live always in an atmosphere of turbulence. He cannot remain alone; he is always looking for company. However, he himself is not a good pal. He believes he is above the others in everything. The girls chase after him, and he is superficial and fickle, always changing his intimate friends.

If we show films to people of George's mentality, they will be taught by the cinema a false picture of the reality of life and will emotionally respond to the cinematic life as seen on the screen, by attempting to live in an atmosphere of ease and these artificial concepts apply to their daily life. This will bring them closer to becoming a future felon in an effort to lead the type of life they see depicted on the screen. A type like George who believes that his family worships money will ignore moral law.

To conclude, George's sad story, he ran away from the

institution where he was imprisoned after stealing some articles that he needed for his trip—such as a leather wallet and money. The police pursued him. After a short time he was apprehended and tried in the Juvenile Court of Justice; when after determining that the boy was 13 years of age and consequently responsible for his actions, he was sentenced to a reform school until he reached legal age.

This was undoubtedly a serious measure but perhaps this would teach him a lesson and invoke a desire for an honorable life such as that every normal person should naturally feel. We strongly doubt that imprisonment will help George; we believe that he is lost; he should have received help before he had a chance to deviate from the straight and narrow path.

We can repeat the utterance of a great statesman who said: "A nation is what its citizens make it." If George's future is hopeless we can try to help other potential Georges; diverting them from taking a wrong fork in the road and at all costs we must try to prevent these people from becoming intoxicated by crime films, glorifying brutality.

If we use a certain amount of discipline, we may congratulate ourselves that we have sustained as useful members of society weak citizens with poor characters and criminal tendencies.

We will now refer to another case of perversion, in accordance with documentation obtained from the Social Aid Service in Paris. We refer to a girl called Paulette. Her mother was a notorious Parisian street prostitute who was supposed to have been of good family. To earn money and educate two daughters, she sold her body. Paulette was twelve and a mediocre student; she seemed well brought up and most obedient. She had a provocative manner with the boys and when she was not being watched, she was boisterous and vulgar. She was cold by nature, unaffectionate, and lacked all moral sentiment. Her intelligence was of a practical nature, but she was extremely selfish and very petty. She exploited the boys who subjugated their will to hers and she would extort money from, eat their lunches and would even strike them.

She was at time rude to her friends, hitting them, hiding their things and then enjoying the unhappiness her pranks caused. Paulette was a glutton, demanding and thinking only of herself. This young girl of 12, who lived always in misery, had only one desire: to be wealthy and have several servants at her beck and call.

She took advantage of opportunities; she was scheming and sensual. Not being artificial, she had all the characteristics of an unscrupulous woman who turns to prostitution in an effort to satisfy her slothful instincts of desire. Her heartlessness is oblivious to educational influence, and she cannot change. She is a serious threat to the morals of her girl companions and those of the opposite sex.

Under these conditions, nothing can be done except an attempt to restrict her contact with other adolescents, and thus delay as much as possible the occasion when she will have the liberty to satisfy her instincts.

At present in France, only the *Bons Pastores* are in charge of girls like Paulette. They are sheltered until they are of age but as soon as they are on their own, many of them let loose completely; almost making up for the time they were protected. Experience tells us that often efforts to form good character are more important than corrective methods. In Paulette's case it is a bit too late. For other cases, rapid intervention at the time when a bad character is first manifested may be more successful.

It is always easier to prevent than to remedy. Evidently, in this situation, the cinema may provoke a tendency, since by putting certain ideas into children's heads, a serious outcome may result. The dangers that thousands of children are subjected to can be avoided if they are not shown such films.

The cinema is an example of an image that moves and

speaks simultaneously. As we have been able to determine its influence is unlimited; we consequently cannot set frontiers for the torrent of anguished impulses that it provokes without making some distinction between people with neurotic and psychopathic tendencies who attend movies and are not impressed by the images. For a more detailed explanation see the work of Dr. Juliette Boutonier, Professor of Philosophy at the Sorbonne entitled *L'Angoisse* (The Anguish) and published by the French University Press.

If truly criminal acts are related to environment and poor education, as well as to the cinema, then what is required for a child to become a true and happy individual and a useful member of society?

To answer this question we must examine the living conditions of the children who have been abandoned and those whose bad luck or birth prevented their being initiated into the cultural values of the community.

Even though several cases are taken into consideration by the medical profession and then a certain line of treatment is followed, the fact remains that each individual child is different and requires special attention. Each human being has his own individual nature, a result of the particular circumstances of his life and of his surroundings. In the meantime, the thorough study of cases of unhappy children does allow us to distinguish a certain number of causes, always in keeping with the personality and we can affirm that those factors are invariably found in the origin of their lamentable destiny.

We should examine the heredity of these children. Some medical and psychiatric schools regard this factor as all powerful; others are apt to consider the importance of heredity as non-existent. We follow the common sense line saying that beautiful furniture and objects cannot be made unless the materials are good to begin with.

The situation with regard to human beings is not different. Studying the cases of these poor unfortunates, we find that the material from which they were formed was of an inferior quality. All, with few exceptions, are weak and little able to resist disease and their natures are often the end product of, or at least weakened by, the errors of one or more generations. This together with a lack of hygiene, insufficient food and a lack of discipline, will weaken the organism still more and truly harm the results of procreation.

At times, the traces of the degeneration common to corrupted familes were found such as syphilis, tuberculosis, alcoholism. Well, these conditions do not limit their action to weakening the system and diminishing resistance, but augment the suffering produced by intoxication with the movies. All together, they contribute to the weakening of mental faculties and moral dispositions. The children who are morally abandoned, are very often mentally retarded, often organically difficient, and many of them have abnormal characters or are perverse, completely lacking in all moral sentiment. The pathological dispositions and the morbid tendencies that an intelligent education can often control, find a receptive ground for their development in disorganized existence that is the sad privilege of children reared in a bad environment.

Some literary works attempt to show that delinquent children are often superior mentally but completely without virtues. (See the work of Professor Heuyer of Paris on this subject).

On this matter we will enter into greater detail in a separate section, considering weak children simply as another special group.

Let us now cite a case on file from the studies of the Neuropsychiatry Service for young patients of the Hospital for Mentally Ill Children, directed by Dr. Heuyer. Before we discuss another example, we would like to point out that the feeble ones do not remember the films they saw twenty-four hours before—all they remember are the scenes of great emotion that may have made them sad or frightened and with which they will dream at night making their state even worse.

Thus, the studies we are making are carried out through cinematographic tests and psychological examinations. Let us this time call our boy Gabriel. He is twelve years old, but seems to be only ten. He has a candid expression, like that of a child who has not been mistreated by life. His blue eyes, his blond hair and his light skin reveal his Flemish origin. When he speaks his head and shoulder twitch nervously. When we see his convulsions which are repeated frequently, we feel pity and we have the impression that the boy is tormented by something. He will laugh and speak interminably, always along incomprehensible lines. Gabriel lives in an imaginary world, closed to the outside and he is satisfied with his status. He does not like to be pulled away from his fictitious world and sometimes becomes disagreeable, even violent. To escape from something that he finds unpleasant, he will make believe that he does not know what it is all about. He is so crafty that he always finds a way to get out of any task or homework. He is very unstable in his likes and dislikes and cannot fix his attention on anything. He will experiment, meanwhile, a certain joy during the classes he attends. He is almost able to read and is making progress in spelling and math. He has a kind of plastic memory and can transcribe things with ease but he will quickly forget what he has learned —and the absence of interest makes him completely inattentive. However, this only increases his mental weakness. It is possible that he can be taught, if he has individual care. As regards his aptitudes for social life, Gabriel is not a person who can adjust to daily living because he only likes to play alone and has no wish to mix with the others.

Gabriel is very puerile for his age and has need for affection but he himself is not affectionate, since there is no way to exert an educational influence over him. He had a very unusual past. Gabriel was accused of stealing a bicycle, of almost burning a neighborhood hut and of untying a neighbor's wild dog just for kicks. All the psychologists and neurologists of Paris knew him and agree that he should be placed in a home for mentally retarded children. But the mother can't make up her mind to do that, and while she hesitates, Gabriel continues to be undersirable wherever he goes.

The neighbors complain constantly, until one day Gabriel is jailed after being accused of several crimes. The young psychopath becomes a delinquent. Tormented by his ever-increasing twitches, he becomes dangerous to society. He was held culpable of robberies and vandalism.

Upon being questioned by the judge, he did not understand the commotion around him and continued to live in his dream world. Dr. Heuyer, who was present at the youth's trial, decided to take him to his clinic for mentally sick children. It was there that we had our first contact with Gabriel. His case was reported incurable and the boy stayed in that clinic for eight months and although all the medical resources were applied, no positive results were attained. Once he got out of there, Gabriel joined a band of boys, organized like the "gangs" seen in the movies. After some wild doings and even armed attempts, the police arrested the young delinquents and they were placed in a correctional school. This time, Gabriel's mental state did not serve as an excuse and he was severely punished, as were his companions.

After this occurrence, we never heard anything about the fellow again. Who then should we blame? The unconscientious parents who ignore the terrible law of solidarity that unites generations which at times can have an effect on human emotions like that of a vampire drinking human blood, cheap writers who explore any form of sensational thrill and obscenity, the producers of films that specialize in selling artificial sensations to the highest bidder, leaving behind them fright and anguish united with still greater misery! It is most evident that by combating this condition we will also fight crime and protect the most sacred thing in the world; the justice and liberty of free men.

IV THE CHILD'S REACTION TO THE MOVIES

Chapter 4

THE CHILD'S REACTION
TO THE MOVIES

We are aware of the danger to adolescents from a lurid film or a bad book. One of the secret vices of youth is an obsession with images, whether evoked through written descriptions or filmed scenes. Due to the injurious influence of the images there develops a disequilibrium or imbalance which may bring forth a mental weakness that later will be almost impossible to cure.

If the images were clear, limpid and free of all sentimental suggestion, the harm would not be so great. But every image that evokes a deep emotion, particularly one based on instinct and cloaked in subterfuge, is twice as dangerous. Although movies may be out of the realm of reality, the effect would not necessarily be detrimental. However, the adolescent who sees the film accepts the things he sees at face value and does not doubt their veracity. The imaginary for him becomes real. He lives in a world of conflict and he does not perceive the evident falseness and the lack of truth that is imposed on him by art or would-be art. If we leave him to the influence of this sorcery, the youth will reach a point where his life will become more imagined than real; more suggested state of being than actual.

This is the magic wrought by imagery and emotion but with it comes the beginning of mental deterioration. This qualification is not too strong as we can see today from the results of certain sophisticated types of literature and what is customarily shown on the screens to young children. The world should not be surprised at the crimes of passion, frequently committed by youngsters, where the original impulse was conceived in the movies. For each crime of that type

67

that actually occurs, there are thousands that are dreamt of but are not carried out.

Therefore we should be convinced more than ever of the power of the "sentimentalized" image when we see an adolescent excitedly reading a trashy book or watching a sensational movie. Instead of his being the creator of his own dream world, he ends up by accepting that of others—the image is imposed on him when it should be the other way around. This fictitious dream-world which has no concrete relationship to the world of reality, will cause abnormal behavior in the individual that will be an indication of the mental abnormality of which he is the victim.

The image suggests the act that it represents and is the beginning of the act itself. Reason and will are not free but on the contrary are actually repressed, the unfortunate influence of the image prevents the adolescent from being emancipated early in life from his primitive instincts. Thus, the mind of the individual becomes almost wholly dominated by fantasy patterns that not even maturity can erase. The young fellow grows to manhood but he is still a prisoner of the imagery. At 18, 20, or even 30 years of age he still cannot free himself from that unreal force and may forever remain a slave to it, if a disciplined will is not developed.

Very few of these images have the power of suggestion for good. The greater number of them have a potential for harm that makes it difficult even for an adult to free himself completely from their yoke. The person who lives on false images and entertains himself with them is truly selfish because, by enclosing himself in a fictitious world, he cuts himself off from the outside world. Nothing else interests him as he is captivated by the moving image which completely dominates him to the point of addiction. No other person exists for him, because of the fear of the destruction of his artificial existence.

It is evident that we cannot ban debased literature, nor

prohibit the exhibition of such films. This would be impossible. It is not by repudiating these dangerous novels and films, or by refusing all stimulus to the imagination and sensibility of the adolescent, that he will acquire a healthful moral development. This would contribute, on the contrary, to warping him morally and exasperating him to a different state, perhaps even more dangerously acute. The excitement denied him will be sought after but in a more furtive way. The specific dosage that each individual can tolerate must be previously determined and really involves in a last analysis, a question of discretion. It is important to point out that the truly moral aspect of the problem is, no matter how strange it may seem, secondary.

In effect, if the film is harmful, it is because it weakens the mind. This is what must be avoided—the type of debilitating factor that is pernicious. If this can be done, living under damaging influences ceases to be a problem or at least, their effects will be diminished.

The power of the cinema, even when good and healthful, can cause a kind of psychological enfeeblement that, in the case of an adolescent, may result in a failure to comprehend unrelated subjects. The question of specific tolerance is something that we cannot answer unless we know the patient. It is also evident that if an adolescent goes to the cinema at least four or more times a week, the dosage cannot be reduced suddenly, without the person's facing a rapid and dangerous change with unforeseen consquences to his mental structure. We do not see how, under the spell of images producing a fictitious concept of life, the individual can progress and become integrated in the world of reality and in the midst of which he must learn how to act.

Daily we see cases of men, influenced by the harmful effect of the movies, expressing erroneous ideas and false judgments or superficial views, on women, love, marriage, family and the meaning of life.

It is necessary that parents take the education of the children in charge and be wholly conscious of their responsibility.

Parents should analyze movies that the children want to see. If harmful they must prevent their children from attending. If doubtful or even good, they should not permit too frequent attendance. Let them explain to the children why this or that film is offensive or false, and why it does not reflect real life. From this type of conversation will develop a true intimacy between parents and children and this intimacy of the child with its parents will grow into a profound affection that will allow a deep understanding and a mutual trust, giving the father greater educational and psychological control whereby he can direct the children without filial rebellion. That clearly will help the parents to protect the children from the dangers of everyday life and more specifically, will contribute as a genuine preventative against the abuses of films. We all like motion pictures for the entertainment they provide. They make us forget the troubles of daily life. But the child, who worries on a more limited scale, does not need the stimulus of images. Let us then leave the cinema to adults, who are less susceptible to its influence than adolescents.

We can say truly that cinematographic images aid the mind of the adult to reach an equilibrium somewhere between the real and the fictitious. On the other hand, to the adolescent technical artifices, cardboard scenery, glycerine tears, and forced smiles make an impression that he accepts as fully valid and gives him a false picture of life. If the adult could return to his childhood he would probably discover that what shaped his life and gave him a true impression, were not the kind of images saturated with sentiment, that are found in books and movies.

The potency of the motion picture image frequently is stronger than that produced by a book. Very often we will retain in our memories an image from the former source, retaining it for many years, without forgetting the smallest detail. And perhaps we would not be what we are today, if in order to give substance to our wishes and make them materialize before our eyes, we had not been encouraged by the life story of some great man, whose example was worthy of emulation.

Parents must help the children to combat the false images brought to them by unhealthy movies and poor books. In this way, they will be participating in a great offensive in the fight on juvenile delinquency, now such a malignant element in our civilization, where the principal factors responsible for the high degree of criminal actions of the youth can be found in the movies, television, the psychology of the cold war, the poverty of innumerable countries and the poor examples set by the parents themselves and by the people with whom they associate.

It has been definitely determined that darkness facilitates crime and it is very certain that the night and the shadows are more propitious to thoughts as well as to acts that are usually held in check. The dark auditorium of the cinema does foster that inspiration to crime and improper thoughts. Dr. Juliette Boutonier in her work *L'Angoisse* (Anguish) wrote:

"Isn't it always at night that the girl will dream by her window that her timid lover will dare to sing or serenade her under her balcony? Truly, there is a state of mind that is not that of darkness but of moonlight, that false light, authentically of dreams, where confessions rise to the lips and where love is revealed at a magical hidden moment." The writer even goes beyond that, stating in another passage:

"Darkness is conducive to daring and at times unspeakable thoughts . . . those that hide in the dark, like murderers, in truth are most stimulating to criminal action. If moonlight does exalt love, the shadow of the theatre represses feelings of sexual insecurity and the spectators have a need of that darkness in order to have the illusion that they are in possession of their senses. In this way, the timid ones can truly take advantage of the night. In fact, most human beings will seek darkness to complete the sexual act and we cannot believe that this is only due to habit or to avoid detection—there is an exigency that have its roots in instinct."

Juliette Boutonier concludes her work with the statement:

"Man has one kind of life at night and another during the day; the former being more secretive, more mysterious. This reality can be transformed into the odd belief in the existence of werewolves, those odd creatures that are human by day and become monsters at night." The conclusions presented by the writer are certainly simple and clear.

According to Jung, a child does not retain any details in his imagination when he is told something or when he sees a movie, unless it corresponds to his secret aspirations. Jung illustrates this by referring to the case of two girls who were informed of all the details pertaining to the birth of a child. The course of instruction was completed by a film exhibit on the subject. In spite of all their training, the girls insisted on holding to their own fantastic conception of what really occurred, and Jung concluded:

"If the fantastic and mythological explanation to which the child almost unfailingly gives preference does not answer his wishes in a better way than the scientific explanation, which is the actual one, then undoubtedly there is a risk of closing all accessible means to the child through the channels of imagination."

Then, if the children are so ready to retain fantasies to such a point that the simple relating of an incident may leave an indelible imprint on their minds, it is necessary to admit that there is a need for fantasy. This and similar make-believe needs in our time and in our society are commonplace. All this occurs because of a fascination with werewolves, vampires, frankensteins, witches, phantoms or the devil. It is impressive to see the intensity—almost completely hallucinative—of images of beings that are not real, the importance of which should be minimal in comparison with the importance of real objects that should hold the attention of a child. And when we see the patient work of the parents, who try to bring up a child in an atmosphere of security and kindness, destroyed in a few minutes by a terrible story re-told by a domestic or some friend, we ask ourselves privately whether there are not definite hereditary and mental facets of vulnerable human beings that we could compare and discern as on the diagram of a skeleton, where the permanent deformities may show up when children are undernourished or have very bad hygienic habits.

For example, the fear of being mutilated, of having some part of the body cut is so deeply felt and so intense, that it frightens all of us. Thus, a little girl of ten who was very much afraid of her mother, had among her toys a book of "moralizing" pictures that her parents had bought for her. In the book, the story that most impressed the child was one of a boy who always put his hands in his mouth, no matter how many warnings he got from the parents, until finally a person bearing wonderful gifts appeared and cut his fingers off. Each time the child had the book in her hand, she would ask, insistently why were the fingers of the little boy cut off? Did it really happen?

Though such a child could have had no experience with wounds made with a sharp instrument, nothing can explain her particular sensitivity upon observing the image, unless it was a kind of innate disposition to that practice well-known to adults, onanism. Later, the image in the books attained still greater importance in the mind of the young girl and her nervousness becomes more and more disturbing. Thus, the girl's reaction was due only to an image in a book that was supposed to be for children.

Analogously then, we can realize the danger that a series of moving images as seen on the screen represent to a child. Let us take for example a film like *Beauty and the Beast* with its bloody and sadistic scenes. It fools parents and teachers with its innocent title yet provokes, even in cities like Paris, serious consequences in the minds of the children who go to see it. This is also true in the case of teen-agers and sometimes even adults who view "Westerns" or "cops and robbers" pictures showing gangsters at their criminal work. These films can bring about consequences that last a life time. And that is why critics have called the cinema a magnificent invention with diabolical powers. This in fact is noticed even in fairy-tales as well as in the harmful films or in books, especially those with a moral, that give us the best examples of symbols in which the child sees death as something that will devour him, burn him, even drown him as he associates himself involuntarily with the heroes of the stories that he reads or hears about.

The sadistic imagination of the adult is also a strong instructive factor, since with a surprising assurance it can speak the language of the child, who can understand and is inspired with a terror of death. Truly, the fear of being devoured or killed constitutes a horror that exists in human creatures from tender youth to extreme old age but the movies induce an exaggeration of this natural fear. The movies, above all, the trashy movies, are responsible for the exaggeration of that fear which strikes the mind with greatest intensity after some accident or traumatic shock. The adult and above all, the childish mind, will then evoke an unreal assessment of the situation with anxiety-provoking images.

It is not, however, inadvisable for the young person to become familiar with the emotions of risk; in fact, it would be absurd and dangerous to prevent him from facing a certain amount of anguish, caused by fright and by the attraction of the unkown, which is a necessary conditioning for his development and his discovery of himself and the world. Everyone has the right to a certain amount of sentiment but abuse along those lines can be catastrophic and even more so for a child who faces life without a preconception, without knowing about fear or the sensation of terror. We think it is interesting to mention the experiment of Robert Desoille based on psychoanalysis, with the assistance of the movies. It is very clear that a film that interests us and which we react to emotionally in the magical darkness of the theatre, transports us to a fictitious world and hypnotizes us subconsciously.

Desoille's technique consists in letting the person lie down on a couch, immediately after viewing the film, close his eyes and describe the images that evoke in him reactions from a film as suggested by the experimentor. In the course of the explorations, the patient finds, sooner or later, images that cause distress which therapeutic treatment will help him to face, whether it be by suggestion that he pass on to another phase in his mental outlook, or whether it be by supplying a basis for removing this image from his fear-ridden mind.

This change of phase or level, frequently has as a result the transformation of the forbidden image into another image of a more therapeutic character, the significance of which is clearer.

The object of the technique is not really to overcome the images and calm the patient—as that can be only temporary— the idea is to help him face his anxiety penetrating into his mind and discovering to what depth the roots of such images penetrate.

When the patient becomes conscious of the causes of his fear, the harm and the anxiety tend to disappear because the danger that justifies it doesn't actually exist. As in the course of psychoanalytic treatment, in Desoille's technique, anxiety maybe provoked in the course of the sessions but the person does not suffer constantly. However this eventuality is rare,

and we must assume this small and insignificant risk to find
the cause of the illness of a patient, who suffers from certain
types of mental affliction, such as fascination with images,
acute nervousness or even sexual impotency to a limited degree.

Thanks to this method, we may find the cause of a dis-
tress-provoking image in some occurrence that does not have
a damaging appearance, in the past life of the individual, which
seemed to have no importance for him at the moment when
it occurred. Only some time after the event do the consequences appear. Thereafter, they may affect him for his entire
life. In some cases, the individual may be cured if he receives
appropriate treatment by a competent psychoanalist.

If these psychoanalytical experiences were studied by film
producers, they certainly would learn what the advisable
types of films to be shown should be, and naturally, humanity
could not help but profit from the production of films of
quality and the abandonment of films that have to do with
obscenity, vulgar comedy and vivid scenes of bloodshed and
would thus diminish the constant struggle faced by psychiatrists, doctors, social workers, judges and all those specialized
functionaries of our society, who have to enforce justice and
isolate individuals who try to violate juridical and moral codes.
It would be wise if a producer before making a film, would
consult specialists regarding the influences that the new film
could have on the spectators. It would be still better if each
studio had two or three such specialists on their staff and
thus there would be fewer crimes of passion, mental patients,
and disorders caused by cinematographic images.

We would like to refer to the case of a young woman of
seventeen who saw an erotic film of the *Naked Woman* type.
Although she was mentally sane, she consciously committed
two incredible acts: she defecated right in the office where she
worked and then did it again in her home. It is true that this
girl was preoccupied with a familiar type of conflict neurosis
that had become increasingly serious in recent years, but

the truth is that the influence of the cinema was responsible for provoking such vulgar and shocking acts. Many other tendencies are brought to light by the influence of images. Let us see, for example, the case of the individual who has aggressive and destructive instincts. These are manifested frequently, not only toward his fellowman, but also toward inanimate objects, impelling him to destroy something of value.

Children also deface wallpaper or destroy their toys. And if they soil something before destroying it, they derive still greater pleasure and joy. These tendencies are noted at all ages. Children at play on the street and in school, deface the walls, put whiskers on pin-up girls and write pornographic phrases in their school books. Even men will write unprintable words in the urinals, sometimes referring to famous people or to mere acquaintances. Naturally, all these tendencies are brought about by some factor and it is not difficult to discover that this factor derives from the movies and offensive books. And so human beings make known the secret forces that exist in their subconscious. Through a sensational scene or a cruel and bloody episode, that we sometimes view in a film, we see the nature of our instincts with sadistic overtones. At first hand these instincts are possessed by everyone in varied degrees. After an initial experience, at times there will be a complete change in the habit patterns of the individual, depending on his adaptation to his environment and on his self-control. There are instances when after a strong emotion evoked by the cinema or even by another source, this may cause adults to bite their tongue or lips until blood comes or dig their nails to the palms of their hands. In this last instance, the mechanism of their reaction seems very clear because it is known that this reaction is produced only when a strong feeling of aggression against an exterior object is contained or repressed. Thus energies could be mobilized to attack any individual who might stand in the way, when the way is blocked for a nervous release.

Let us quote here the film *The Eternal Return* (L'Éternel Retour) a very successful film which is an example of the persistence through the centuries of the Tristan & Isolde legend that demonstrates the undiminished influence and the power it exerts on the masses. Tradition is not the only factor to blame for human weakness as regards images. After some study it was discovered that a high percentage of the people who went to see *Tristan* & *Isolde* had no knowledge of the traditional romance and it was verified that their reaction was not on an adult level, though there is no doubt that a well-educated individual would be familiar with the episodes of the story. Thus even a classic story can, in the medium of the cinema, provoke a damaging reaction.

We see also the case of a girl of sixteen completely influenced by this film because all the movies she had previously seen had failed to awaken her sensuality. This is an eternal theme, as the title of the film itself seems to emphasize, and it remains in the hearts of men even after middle age with the same surprising force of dominant sensation.

What shocks the public most, evidently, are not the details of a legend but the last scene of the film with death as the final end and destiny of love. The adaptation of this theme in a number of motion pictures results in the increase of similar reactions.

Another film that was very successful in France was held over in the theatre for a full year. The story concerned a man who was faithful to his lost love, tormented by the remembrance of the wife who had abandoned him and refusing then to start life again in the company of a young woman who loved him, in the little city to which he had moved in the hopes of forgetting everything. In vain did an aged friend try to convince him that each life has a certain destiny and that in each man there is a seed that he himself must nurture. The main character here persisted in the fixed idea of keeping company only with the phantom that joined him with his broken love. This theme, which was also very successful as a play, under the title *The End of the Road* (Le Bout de la Route) based on the play of Jean Giono shows us that while artistic value may not be the main factor responsible for success in the cinema or the theatre, it can be inherent in the work. Thus we come to the conclusion that everything that may impress the public is apt to be transformed into a theatrical or cinematic work although it may not even remotely resemble art. What matters is that there be a love story, a bloody battle with scenes of suspense and a certain coordination in the sequence of emotions. In this manner the success of the film is guaranteed in our present human society containing many sadists, homosexuals and impotent beings. If a film offers a different type of message, a new idea, a novel type of realism, it will not be understood by those accustomed to maintaining a sordid attitude. To the sadist, who cannot give vent to his feelings only—after all, we can't all be Hitlers and Himmlers—the darkened theatre represents their field of action. For two hours their suppressed instincts come to the fore and there they can remain, associating themselves with the film.

In the same way, homosexuals and impotent people of both sexes find there a sublime exaltation, an artificial short-term pleasure, that the normal natural process does not allow them for anatomical or mental reasons, or due to the anxiety and nervousness that commonly dominate them. It was proven in some cases that some impotent human beings are temporarily victims of hypnosis due to the images and acute emotion gets such a hold on them that sexual contact becomes almost impossible. Only psychoanalytic or therapeutic treatment will cure them. This is a subject that has not yet been too well studied by scientists and one cannot write too authoritatively about it.

Now, I would like to refer to another example—a highly successful French film by Jean Anouilh, entitled *Le Voyageur*

Sans Bagage (Voyager without Baggage) dealing with a soldier who has suffered an amnesia attack during World War I, immediately after being wounded. He completely forgot all about his family and his past. When he found himself again in the region where he lived and saw his real "background," he could see that actually he had been a cruel cynic, living with a family that had little to recommend it. The sensitive, tender being he had become after being wounded by the war was so different that he became confused, after many revelations, and, as a result, preferred to continue on as he was, alone, away from the falseness of his family; and thus he continued for the rest of his days, leading the new life he had chosen for himself.

This disturbing story fills us with profound emotion because we all have our own crosses to bear in life. How many of us wish we could start from the beginning and abandon our present lot? Many neurotic and disturbed individuals could thus forget their childhood which left such deep scars on them. But all Jean Anouilh does is to illustrate a theme that is very much alive in the conscious or subconscious of his contemporaries. In the motion picture audience there are many nervous individuals who see on the screen a reflection of their emotions, and they live in that sphere, identifying themselves with each of the characters in the films they attend. Therefore we can easily imagine the consequences of the story. No one can forget his own existence and the events in his life, even though he tries to obliterate the past.

Life is much more complicated than that; there is no traveler without baggage because he is always tormented by something, even if it is only the desire to flee from someone. No one's past can be trampled down like a plant, and if tomorrow mankind wants to forget the heavy burden it has carried through the milleniums, it would be necessary to remind every individual in the world that it is not by forgetting that he can attain a better life.

No doubt the conflict that exists between what we are and what we would like to be, generates anxiety but it is not necessary to demonstrate that eternal conflict through motion pictures since this depresses mankind and robs him of courage.

As in the film *Le Voyageur Sans Bagage* (Voyager without Baggage), the false interpretation of daily life will not fail to provide seemingly beneficial examples to the spectator but this is only a short term condition, and illusions will bring greater anxiety afterwards as well as a feeling of defeat and helplessness in his fight against external forces. Thus, due to this sensation, man searches in mountain climbing and other sports for a new world, where pleasure is mixed with mortal risk but that in turn gives him the joy of seeing something new surge around him, attained with his own effort.

The mountain climber always has a large measure of curiosity, of love for adventure and the passionate desire to rise and attain a revelation. And according to P. Dalloz "the appeal of great heights reveals in our soul an immense and instinctive hope, as though infinite possibilities of happiness are open to us."

A man who would try to conquer fear by himself has no need of the cinema to help him artificially since it may often give him the sensation of anxiety that is one of the characteristics of fear. This man by-passes the barrier of anxiety by controlling his fear that impedes him from assuming by himself the responsibility for his destiny; he finds in moments of great risks, that he completely accepts, pleasure and the meaning of his true destiny and thus there is nothing alien to him about himself.

V THE RELATIONSHIP BETWEEN MURDER AND TRAGEDY IN THE MODERN CINEMA

Chapter 5

THE RELATIONSHIP BETWEEN MURDER AND TRAGEDY IN THE MODERN CINEMA

In the words of Roland Caillois, Professor at the University of the Sorbonne, it is clear that homicide in the cinema was soft-pedaled only with difficulty, and only because of the extraordinary power of blood scenes where brutal physical images exert a force beyond anything else on the screen.

Homicide has a spell-binding quality. Some of the most distinguished examples of the cinema are based on themes of homicide. Some of the stories are more effective in the cinematic sense than others: for example tales of crimes such as Charlie Chaplin's *Monsieur Verdoux, L'Étrange Crime de Monsieur Lange,* both French productions, and the American film, *The Killers.*

It is true that the cinema is capable of assuming many of the functions of literature. The narration in any case would be much more valid if the film could bring to life the manner in which the investigation is undertaken. There are not many detective films in the true sense of the word. By this we do not mean films about killers, under the pretext of calling it a detective film (homicide and the hunt for assassins) but a film where the solution to the crime along detailed lines is governed by the science of criminology, and is necessary and essential to solve the enigma of a crime. It seems, at times, that the detective type of film should be succesful on the screen because one could then follow the investigation and learn the secrets revealed by police work and thus judge the soundness or unsoundness of the psychology involved.

Above all, the sensational or artistic side of the macabre can find its medium in this type of film. The cinema must dramatize to the maximum but the argument of the police plot man constitute a brake at times. On the other hand, the macabre, the disturbing sensual factor of the film, contrary to the story from which it was taken, becomes on the screen a useless sensation, exerting a negative tendency toward a sensitive and aesthetic reaction on the part of the spectator.

In cinema records, systematic optimism does not prevail with regard to police work against delinquents and criminals. In life, however, justice can often be more corrupt than the crime itself. Therefore justice of this type causes much violence and misery, leading to murder and bodily violence, as well as occasional suicide. Often a story that is filmed is about an actual occurrence. Regarding characters taken from fiction, for example, the series about the fictitious French screen villains, Rouletabille and Maigret, the prototypes of police detectives, charmed the public with their adventures. The cinema accustoms us to many types of heroes; for instance, the tough guy he-man type of hero like Dashiell Hammett's hero, Detective Marlow, who was portrayed by the late Humphrey Bogart, can hold the spectator's interest. The main purpose of these detective stories was to hold the audience in suspense but unfortunately, it was often deemed necessary to focus more attention on the love interest than on the main plot. Thus the love interest temporarily overshadowed the final solution.

Death which in actual life is a paramount occurrence is merely a fleeting moment on the screen. Death in the cinema is not only tragic but often pathetic.

As a result, the spectator experiences from the cinema the physical nature of death, even though unreal and imaginary; he can be actually intoxicated by the sensation of pain imposed on him through scenes of torture, and by physical cruelty in general. We see before our eyes suffering humanity under

French film: THE ETERNAL RETURN (*L'eternal Retour*)
Jean Marais and Madeleine Sologne
Directed by Jean Dellanoy

French film: LES LIAISONS DANGEREUSES
Directed by Roger Vadim

Brazilian film: THE OUTLAW *(O Cangaçeiro)*
Milton Ribeiro and Alberto Ruschel
Directed by Lima Barreto

Brazilian film: MISSY *(Sinhá Moça)*
Eliane Lage
Directed by Tom Payne

Brazilian film: BEACHCOMBER *(Caiçara)*
Directed by Adolfo Celi

Brazilian-French film: BLACK ORPHEUS *(Orfeo Negro)*
Breno Mello and Marpessa Dawn
Directed by Marcel Camus

Russian film: THE RAINBOW *(Raduga)* Stalin Prize 1944
Natasha Uzhevy
Directed by Mark Donskoy

Swedish film: ONE SUMMER OF HAPPINESS *(Hon Dansade en Sommar)*
Ulla Jacobsson and Folke Sundquist
Directed by Arne Mattsson

the most concrete circumstances in the image of murder, the temporary anguish of death but actually not the full impact of it—while the images pass before us on the screen, we react and think as though there had been an actual occurrence. That is why some films can give us a passing feeling of terror, a sharp sensation, to end of which is not terminated with the cinema performance but remains with the individual after he leaves the theatre.

It is at this moment that the individual, of whatever age, is capable of all kinds of irrational acts in accordance with the circumstances that he encounters because his mind does not yet have the elasticity to think and direct his conduct in the normal mental pattern. On the screen, the world seems to be satirical in its details, due to the numerous rough scenes portrayed. While attempting to be over-perfect, the assassin usually forgets at least one important detail which in the end is often the key to his being discovered.

We must reserve a place of honor for the theme of justice and the punishment of the crime. Actually crime solution in real life is not as efficient nor as easy to solve as it is portrayed on the screen. Such is man's justice: the actual deed is stronger than society itself. The guilty one goes to jail due to the machinations of justice that have nothing of the abstract nor super-human. The witnesses in court react like average human beings, yet they are innocently cruel. The cinema shows magnificently the significance that a tragic scene can convey. But it has to do this with a pathetic sense of the tragedy of life and thus we regard it as a fictitious world. It must be said that the cinema does not do justice to that which is tragic because it shows us man in unusual surroundings awaiting human decision.

Society condemns homicide. It is not enough to punish in the name of morality; it also must persuade us that society sets the pattern and is the judge.

"Crime does not pay" was the theme in a series of American

films. The thought they were trying to get across was—why kill, why disturb the established order of things since you will be only harming yourself by nurturing crime and making it an everyday occurrence?

Guilt and innocence are cinema problems as in the film *The Count of Monte Cristo* where the hero goes after justice in spite of numerous obstructions and where, as a marked man, he has to face the vengeance of an irate group, attempting to corrupt him. It is then that the audience feels identified with the action to the point of intoxication.

The hero—just avenger or criminal—does not attain the unreal grandeur of the tragic hero but the ambiguous reality of myth. What feelings can be evoked by the type of character portrayed by Paul Muni in *Scarface?* We do not know whether to condemn the man or pardon him.

The cinema can be very strict and a definite disciplinarian in following certain points but indulgent in other points that may engender evil.

The cinema is without a doubt the art that deals most profoundly with life, because it is very close to it. Thus, it is the greatest creator of modern myths. That is precisely why it is dangerous: it will excuse certain important things and then show effectively a very modern style that may become perverse to the imagination: it shows how easy it is to kill, that murder is a way out, that it solves certain otherwise insoluble problems. One can say that the cinema has brought little that is new to the world. We all know what life is but the cinema highlights these matters; the reactions of the hero are engraved on our minds; the gestures of the villain are impressive but the latter do not portray real beings in the cinema performances and the interpretation suffers. The theatre really seems strangely abstract as compared to the films where in the majority of screen fare, the revolver is a kind of symbol.

The strength of the stage drama lies in accepting fiction

and re-using it as a basic foundation. On the other hand, the cinema concentrates on what actually takes place. The plots of the theatre are more powerful than those depicted on the screen. In the cinema it is essential that one react to the image; death is not an essential end but a tragic event. The cinema has the ability to expand and augment the themes on human relations. The screen can depict blood-curdling scenes, such as those in *Quo Vadis* and *Fabiola*, where the heroes are faced with a martyr's death in man-to-man or man-to-beast combat in an open arena and are jeered at by a clamoring mob. In real life an innocent bystander may be killed by a gangster because he happened to be in the way; the world has no order; it is a place of chance encounter and haphazard action. At times some sort of regimentation will attempt to impose its set of rules, but in human enterprise it is not always a question of destiny but of opportunity.

Nevertheless, even if the movies may attain some day the tragic quality that is so poignant on the stage, the fact remains that audiences are involuntary victims of criminal action. That is why Bie de Louvain, the French writer, shows us the difference between the traditional arts, such as literature and painting, and the cinema. He points out: "This identification is never a relative sign and it is considerably reduced by the perceptive contact. In this same way these arts exert a function and induce healthy psychological attitudes." In presenting a work on the screen, there is a perfect imitation and one gets the illusion that what is depicted really exists. In fact, the effect is so strong that one can actually experience sensual emotions. The spectator identifies himself with the action on the screen. The individual "lives" the action much more than he contemplates it and tends not to forget the moment when he lives it vicariously, with his fictional character.

When the movie is over, the spectator is torn away brusquely from a fictitious life through which he seemed to live, although in fact, very often it is a life more drab than his own. There is a period of fleeting depression which may become chronic by repetitious viewing of such films and then the individual cannot see any other remedy, except to view more and more films of this type.

These are the psychological characteristics of a person in a toxic condition. Let me just mention as an example, the contrast between the simple life of a laborer and the luxurious and easy life that is often represented on the screen. Dissatisfactions and imperfections of real love seem disappointing compared to the fictitiously perfect love scenes between lovers, couples and parents on the screen. In numerous instances of this type, the cinema offers for the real difficulties of life the subjective equivalent of a satisfying life which invokes a compelling desire on the part of the spectator to project himself into a world of make believe.

European Professors Munsterberg, Zonill and Meurann concluded after their experiments that sound and colors are factors of elementary excitation and provoke interesting reactions in the audience. The results obtained indicate that mental attitudes of a predetermined public can be altered. These audience reactions have the same interest as the tests conducted by commercial publicity which also focuses on a preconditioned group.

Under such conditions, it is easy to see whether the audience reacts to the film in accordance with the intention of the author in predetermined areas.

This method has a value of practical application. The film can react very powerfully on actual life because of the feeling of reality since due to the three-dimensional movement in space, it shows an action that can appear very real and thus, very intense. It is permissable to ask whether certain films do not evoke in us a complex feeling that constitutes the essential conviction of reality. The movies can hypnotize the individual as effectively as an actual hypnotist. Therefore we believe that it is necessary to determine some of the psychological reasons for the great success of the movies among the masses. The psychological qualities of the cinema have already attracted attention and could equally permit the interpretation of the phenomenon of illusions that develop as the movie progresses. In a sense the audience can actually hear the noise of the oars as they cut through the water and simultaneously observe the rowers in action. Ponzo, the Italian specialist, compared analogous auto-observations but he did not interpret them in the same manner as we do. We must yet compare the preponderant role that appears in comics with the exterior elements—gestures, attitudes and positions that awaken in us above all, the comic sense. This humorous trend seems to explain the success of certain American or British comedies. Comic films have great entertainment power and dramatic films provoke strong emotions in people.

We have seen that the respiratory rhythm provoked by a dramatic film persists for some minutes afterwards when a documentary film goes on. From the pedagogical point of view, the psychological studies of the films that are used in schools would be extremely useful, because they would show the degree of interest held in a documentary.

The study completed by Professor D. W. Harding of London, showed through studies made in recent years that even adults can get confused by the manner in which fiction is presented, especially if the film is very realistic and has scenes that are true to life or applicable to their own. There are tendencies—and these were particularly noted among the film audience spectators—to fail to distinguish in a clear and definite way between the actor and the type of role he portrays. An understanding of conventional fiction is not always attained by young people but at the present time we don't know enough about the development of this comprehension or know with assurance what level is attained at different ages. Professor F. C. Bartlett of Cambridge University also tells us that the number of people who are affected is considerable and that the reaction is based on special or characteristic effects of a film particularly its humor, or its horror, in the scenes from typical gangster films. Some even believe that the films produce, in general, identical effects, whatever may be the style of acting and the way in which the sequence ends.

Some think that the effects are completely transformed by the manner in which these sequences are connected. Everything depends, they say, on the moral of the story or the sex of the spectator. The great number of people who go to the movies will see many films and we do not know how they react to each one. The results of these reactions are a complex of conventions and this could completely invalidate the deductions of an observant critic concentrating totally or principally on films. The method is to make films, present them to a selective group, and then discuss with these people what they saw.

The crucial inferences of this type of survey in order to have scientific value should be determined by getting the reactions of the different groups and compiling a statistical report on the basis of these observations.

VI AFRICAN MOVIE PROBLEMS

Chapter 6

AFRICAN MOVIE PROBLEMS

We have some comments about the special public of the Congo, which is mostly Negro. Mr. L. Van Bever, then of the Belgian Congo General Government, with the help of Mr. L. Peron, Director of the Secretariat of the same administration, made an interesting study that I will attempt to interpret. This work was published in *Cahiers Belges et Congolais* of 1950, printed in Brussels. The value of the movie as a privileged medium of expression, as a technique for the diffusion of information and education, is no longer under discussion. Experience has proved its worth and the specialists on colonial problems do no more than confirm its efficacy.

Mr. L. Peron tells us: "The study of the public reactions, corroborated by the results of analogous experiences in neighboring territories, leads one to a misleading conclusion. The African, in general, is not mature enough for the cinema, because cinematographic conventions puzzle him; psychological nuances escape his perception; the rapid succession of sequences confuse him. The lack of ability of the African to understand the films is due to a fundamental difference of mentality and civilization as compared with the "civilized" public, whose cinematographic education has progressed for over half a century with variable results both good and bad.

In certain cases one has the impression that this education instead of aiding progress represents a great step backwards, thus retarding education and where we believe it educates, it actually stupefies.

In the same way, John Maddison of the *Colonial Film Unit* of Great Britain, with a wealth of material and lengthy documentation, proves that in the Colonies of Great Britain

95

most of the African Negroes are also not sufficiently prepared for the cinema to be prevented from being injured mentally or from misunderstanding the moving images.

In a work published in the *Revue de Filmologie*, No. 4, Vol. I, Mr. Maddison praises the use of movies with the African peoples, but suggests a cinema adapted to the public to which it is directed: One that has as a background the African landscape, that use local talents, that shortens the length of the films and gives a definite slow rhythm to the sequence.

This subject will be studied later for a better idea of its application. The movie is the most powerful medium of expression ever discovered by man. More powerful even than the press because for that one must know how to real. However, this skill is not necessary for visual observation. It is more powerful than the radio, because it is necessary to know the language that one hears to understand a radio broadcast.

The cinema is the "visual esperanto," the universal language that directs itself to all eyes, speaking in understandable language to all people. This is the universal language that the African Negroes need, the ideal instrument, the best medium offered for the education of these primitive people.

The education of the masses in its broadest sense, should have as its objective the helping of the primitive populations to reach a standard of life in accordance with the conditions of their status and environment, to develop their own culture and to reach a higher economic and social level.

If it is true that the efforts of the educators should be directed to more than the mere teaching of reading and writing, then in that case the cinema can be the educator for the African population and if it is used honestly, in the full sense of the word, it is a fine method of teaching.

As a matter of fact, the cinema does not ask of the spectators any effort other than that of "looking." It can teach the illiterate primitive communities how to fight disease, obtain better crops and how to build better houses. All this can be taught without forcing them to go through the initial chores of learning to read and write.

In this way, using tactfulness with the masses, and adapting its technique to the mentality and social levels of the spectators, the cinema can produce great results toward the development of modern civilization among this people. There is no doubt that the cinema is not an instrument to be used indifferently by any one and in any way.

If the films remain completely in the hands of private groups, the latter, caring little about the education and reactions of the Africans, may completely disturb the Negroes' intelligence which is not yet used to the cruelties of so-called "civilized" life with all its trappings.

Furthermore a film can cause various mental and sexual deviations, thus inducing the possibilities of murder and robbery. On the other hand for private groups of exploiters and producers, the only concern is that of their commercial profits without any regard for other types of problems.

All standard methods, all the conventions of cinematographic language used to establish time, unity and place, that to us seem normal and of which we no longer take much notice, can completely upset an unsophisticated and primitive public. The public will conclude, seeing the dissolves and the "fade outs" of the scenes that the cinema equipment is not in order. A diagram does not suggest anything to someone who is not sufficiently instructed to find through a convention of lines and forms the object that is being explained. In the case of vertical, horizontal or oblique "panning," the moving camera only serves to confuse them. They will not understand that it is the camera that moves. They see trees moving on the screen; constructions go up and down, objects in motion that normally should not move.

The attention of the Negroes is distracted from the action

of the film. Sometimes they even believe they are being made fun of since they do not have the capacity to distinguish the difference between reality and the artificial technique of the cinema and therefore they get angry and throw objects at the screen. All the conventional tricks of modern cinema are of understandable scope to a prepared public, but meaning nothing to a primitive audience it is necessary to teach them how to understand the images.

John Maddison, whom we quoted above, proposes for the African public simple pictures where they can find elements at their own level: water, fire, soil, a house, plants, animals. When the African has acquired the habit of seeing and understanding simple pictures, it will not be difficult to add an action, a person or several persons. Little by little better use of these elements can be made. Nevertheless, such a method should not be static. On the contrary, it should undergo a constant evolution. The introduction to cinematographic conventions must be made carefully and at the same time the introduction to the pictures should tend toward a gradual adaption of modern movie techniques.

Some native Africans, who through contact with our civilization have acquired other needs and tendencies, while still having deep-seated roots in their environment, are inclined to adapt our methods and customs. For this public, generally very heterogeneous, the film should nevertheless preserve simplicity in order to be understood by all the viewers.

By simple films we mean films photographed in natural backgrounds, stripped of any cinematographic tricks. The shots should be taken at eye level, with the least possible movement of the camera and reproducing faithfully what the human eye sees. The maximum possible visual continuity should be maintained from scene to scene. Persons or objects requiring attention should be seen again in the following picture. Applying this principle will allow for much clearer understanding of the action and eliminate a great number of sub-titles otherwise needed as explanation. A minimum number of actors should be used because a great number of people on the screen will confuse the viewer. The film should consist almost entirely of long shots or medium close-ups and in much longer sequences than those we are used to see made with normal techniques. At the intellectual level they need more time to understand, to "digest" each picture, and series of pictures. For the same reason the sub-titles, in short and easy sentences, should remain on the screen twice the time needed for normal reading. Our European educational films provoke in the African at most curiosity if not indifference. However, show him a film on the same subject but in a setting familiar to him, acted out by someone of his own race and curiosity will change into comprehension and indifference into enthusiasm. Let us show him different aspects of his own or other countries, but let the film be lively. Let us tell a short and plausible story with an actor of his own race, with whom he can identify himself and avoid changing scenery, and paraphernalia. The African does not like to look hurriedly at many things at the same time; he loves details . . . give him close-ups and enough time to see well, assimilate each gesture. He will watch, with attention and a critical mind, an artisan of his own race (shoemaker, carpenter, blacksmith) make a pair of shoes, a chair or an axe. Since the narrative style is familiar to African culture, the film should take the form of a tale. Stories adapted from native folklore will furnish plently of material. Satirical subjects, with native actors, of course, will also have a chance for success. Music has an important place in the life of the native African population who use it at every opportunity with or without reason, whether they are at work or are resting.

They find it difficult to work without the accompaniment of their native rhythms. To the African, music is a part of his life. It is natural for him to participate in it even without listening. Therefore, a movie with musical accompaniment has a much better chance to please the African public than a silent one.

Nevertheless we must not suppose that music is universal and that our music is as pleasant to the Africans as it is to us. Does it please them? Haven't we sometimes heard in the movies or over the radio or even on the street Hindu or Arab music? I remember that during the five years that I spent in Africa I was often obliged to close the window in order to shut out the music that seemed like an orchestra from Hades but which the natives themselves would not exchange for the best Western concert orchestra. As you see—to each his own!

English, Italian and French producers have thought of using Japanese or Chinese musical accompaniments in their films with sequences from these countries. Therefore we can use African music in the films to be distributed in Africa. The actors of educational films must be, whenever possible, native Africans. It is not too easy to find good interpreters. The African is a born actor and he differs from the European in an essential point: there is a complete absence of timidity and embarrassment. His acting is entirely natural and his sense of humor well developed. He never gets confused with his hands nor does he make facial grimaces. At times he must act with certain rapidity or then again, in a sort of slow motion, he will exaggerate his gestures. However, it will be easy to correct these mannerisms.

The African woman, on the contrary, is a timid, artificial, being. One can never definitely count on her. There are cases where, after a difficult search, one can find an African woman who will accept a role in a film. One can instruct her and make her rehearse her role—in fact, one can complete more than half the takes when—without any reason at all, our improvised actress will refuse adamantly to continue the work . . . all the cajoling, pleadings, all the offers of an increase in salary are in vain; nothing can change her stand and nothing can be done. In case women are necessary for a certain role in the film, the best thing to do is to turn to an African who already has had European training—the Director of a School or a Mission, or even a nurse.

It is not any easier to try and get a natural portrayal from African children unless the action is within their normal behavior pattern or daily routine. In general the boys are better actors than the girls.

If we show cinemascope, 3D or the common black and white film to the Africans who never before saw stills—that is, that which they are not accustomed to seeing around them —still, frozen, crystalized life—it will be the same as taking the wrong fork in the road. How can they accept the image of a water fall when the water does not move—or then— a bird stopped in flight? Wouldn't it be more simple, more efficient to them than the images, to show them a river that runs, waters that ripple, birds that fly?

Professor Julian Huxley has reached the same conclusions after his cinema experiments carried out in Kampala, East Africa. He wrote a report upon returning to England, and commented therein:

"All who noted how the primitive native has difficulty in recognizing stills are amazed at the manner in which he can comprehend animated images—such as the cinema."

The education of Africans by images then should from now on be made preferably through the cinema, the only way capable of giving them a faithful representation of life. It is true that for best results the power of the cinema must be controlled through a careful dosage as a preventive measure against cinematographic intoxication, so very easy when directed to a public that is but little civilized and has an inadequate sense of responsibility.

The problem is not only one of the Africans or of the Negroes in general; as was seen, it is the same in the Congo, in the British Commonwealth or in the former French colonies because it does not depend on race or color. It is a problem common to all countries where the inhabitants have always been in a primitive state of civilization, or else, where there is a condition of illiteracy or semi-illiteracy as, for example, in the interior of Brazil and in other countries of South America.

It is obvious that an individual who does not know how to read or write and has never left his native hearth will not understand all the mysteries of technical effects and cinematographic equipment; but this does not constitute a great danger because what he does not understand, he cannot interpret falsely. Thus we can be almost certain that he will not adapt the image of the film to his own life. On the other hand, the semi-illiterate is capable of making a kind of adaptation of cinematographic images to the medium around him and this facilitates the first step toward the road to delinquency where robbery, theft, and even homicide are common occurrences.

As the great criminologists—Lombroso, Ferrara and Pinadel have stated—it is the first conflict with the law that prepares them for future run-ins. It is much more difficult for one "outside the law" to take the right road, once he has strayed from it. What frequently happens is that he will continue to defy law and justice. We are certain that many of the crimes and attacks committed by known semi-illiterates have cinematic origins. A greater control of this field could change the fate of many of those who now go against the law and become future hospital cases or jail-birds.

In regard to Negroes and the cinema, the complex and delicate question of color bigotry handled in a special way in the American cinema has been a topic for a superb series of films. The first, *Home of the Brave,* was a poignant drama, showing racial discrimination in the armed forces of the Pacific during the war and the same theme was used again, with ardent democratic sentiments in films like *Pinky, Lost Boundaries, No Way Out,* and *Intruder in the Dust.* This last mentioned is one of the great works of Hollywood.

It is true that in these films we notice American propaganda, as it is true in all kinds of films of this type, principally on war themes; but this is insignificant, compared to Russian films of the same type. Some of the latter are notable but the propaganda slant is such that movie-goers outside the Iron Curtain are almost suffocated by it.

The Negro problem in America is not exactly as shown in films. It varies in accordance with the area of the country. However, the situation of the colored people in all of North America improved after the Second World War, thanks to the forthright thinking of Presidents Roosevelt, Truman, Eisenhower and Kennedy.

The objective now is to develop equality between whites and blacks in the United States—a "de jure" as well as a "de facto" equality, wherein Moses' prophecy will attain its true meaning—"All men are brothers without regard of race, color or creed."

VII THE CINEMA AS A FORCE FOR INTERNATIONAL UNDERSTANDING

Chapter 7

THE CINEMA AS A FORCE FOR INTERNATIONAL UNDERSTANDING

We have here a commentary by Ross McLean, ex-head of the Film and Visual Information Division of UNESCO, on international understanding and the cinema. If we examine in what way the cinema contributes to international understanding, we will see that it is not only an intellectual medium. It is also part of the special effort we are making with the object of bringing a little harmony to the confused world bequethed to us by humanity. Everyone agrees that films may have the power to amuse, arouse energies, provoke hatred, superstition, pity, or respect. We probably speak more of the movies than the movies speak of themselves because the film, more than any other art form, is in a state of continuous development.

To assert that the cinema is an instrument capable of interpreting life and that it contributes to our hopes for a more harmonious world, does not imply that it should abstain from one of its principal duties, that of entertainment. But in the search for themes, more authors, producers, film directors and actors, should direct their gaze to the barriers that divide humanity, in order to contribute in their proper field toward the orientation of a reasoned way of life, rather than towards passions of death and destruction. Let the themes be joyful or sombre, light or heavy; that does not matter. The barriers that divide humanity are not only the national and political frontiers. There are the barriers of mind and spirit that have as their origin inadequate experience or differences of organization, tradition, beliefs, or taste that are deliberately or accidentally exploited for sinister purposes. That is why so many specialists are preoccupied today with the influence of films on both children and adults.

Our generation may be without hope, but none of us should concede that our children must also be. For them, above all, we must find a drastic remedy for the future, or they will suffer the horrors of the last decade. Whether a film is made in Mexico, Argentina, the United States, in Russia or in the United Kingdom, in France or Italy, in Egypt (U.A.R.) or in India, in Indonesia or in Japan, all have a common obligation to the children of the world. The actual situation does not suggest a propitious and specialized method of carrying out past obligations of research in the mind of the youths, even with a full staff of specialists in the field.

The task is not so easy to carry out. Taboos of all kinds limit our field of action. There are forces that take advantage of the disorder of our divided world, attempting at every step to subjugate the creative spirit. There are also problems of financing facilities and adjustment.

Before we can satisfy our doubt, we must consider the tremendous job of preparation and research. Our hope for the future rests in the constructive collaboration of various people of good sense and moral conscience. For many years it has been a recognized fact that the cinema possesses latent power to transmit concepts, impressions and facts. An example is necessary to demonstrate, among other things, the fact that most of the valid or erroneous ideas that civilized countries have about the American way of life are based in large measure on films produced in Hollywood. A study on this subject made by Stephen Watts, cinema critic of the *New York Times* in London illustrates this point. Documentaries, educational films and war themes, as well as films of present day life all contributed to it. Until now the cinematic efforts have been restricted in this field and it could contribute much more efficiently in the future as an adequate means of international understanding. In the Western World films suspected of propaganda are in general poorly received. But this is not the case in the Eastern hemisphere of the world. Thus, the *Times* of London publishes a report from Singapore referring to the cinematic campaign carried out in Southeast Asia for the diffusion of Russian and Chinese Communist ideology among the masses. We can better appreciate the constructive value of the fiction films, duly documented, after comparing them with sentimental themes the basis of which, in the last analysis, is to make believe that complete happiness can be attained.

Of these relatively scarce films, we can say that human values breed in motion-picture goers a desire to emulate that which they see on the screen.

If films like *Paisan* or *Open City* describe Italy at war in a surprisingly vivid way it is because its producers, poor in equipment but rich in ideas, have chosen subjects of reality and simplicity.

Among the films possessing human values, it is necessary to mention the Austro-Swiss polyglot production *Four in a Jeep* that concerns the quadripartite occupation of Vienna. The Russians, it is true, protested against the showing of that film at the Cannes and Venice Film Festivals, finding without a doubt the principal Soviet character to be insufficiently heroic; but criticism was favorable in Cannes, as well as in London, Venice, and Berlin. Certain critics saw in this film an effort to promote better understanding among human beings and brought to mind the objectives of the Golden Laurel Prize as expressed by its donor, David O. Selznick, who stated: "Giving prizes to films of European production has definitely contributed toward tightening the bonds of friendship and understanding among the peoples of the democratic free world."

I would like to refer to the Golden Laurel Prize which

was established in 1950 to promote better understanding among peoples oblivious to the commercial or mercenary qualities involved.

The First Award Committee with headquarters in New York was composed of such personalities as Dr. Ralph Bunche, Nobel Peace Prize Winner and a member of the United Nations, Herbert Bayard Swope, newspaper editor, Edward R. Murrow, news commentator and present Director of the United States Information Agency, John Gunther, author of the *Inside* series and a member of the Golden Society of New York, and René d'Harnoncourt, Director of the Museum of Modern Art of New York. The first film to win this award was the Franco-Italian production, *Women Without Names* (Les Femmes Sans Nom) which was presented at the Venice Film Festival, and is a moving and dramatic portrayal of women without a country in a camp for displaced people.

Other films that were presented included *Trio*, based on three short stories of Somerset Maugham, a piquant film and full of the humor of the British character. This film will confirm foreign countries in their concept of one of the most charming English idiosyncracies: that of poking fun at themselves. From France we received *Justice is Done* (Justice est Faite) a film that deals with the hesitations of a jury made up of honorable people judging a case of euthanasia. The other Italian film was *The Road to Hope* (Il Camino della Speranza) which shows us poor Sicilian immigrants traveling toward the French frontier in quest of work, after the closing of the sulphur mines in their native town. This simple film portrays true life so beautifully, deals with the valid problems of human feelings, and is, indeed, a realization of life with no technical tricks or artificial suspense—it actually leaves the spectator in a deep state of meditation.

It would be very simple indeed if the producers, instead of presenting the "duds" based on violent emotions, like the Tarzan and Western films, or the various kinds of crime movies, would conserve their efforts to produce films like *While the City Sleeps* (Medan Staden Sover) from Scandinavia or the German language film *Wonderful Times* (Herrliche-Zeiten). In these films the exhilarating element is almost insignificant, contrary to most films.

This competition for the Golden Laurel Award will not fail to stimulate cinematographic production in Europe on a small scale, improving their productions and awakening interest in motion picture producers and directors toward a new aspect of their duties, which they often ignore.

But the principal thing is to educate audiences and promote the culture and motion picture language in order that the people may refuse to see a film if they know it is of poor quality. The Hollywood producer at the proper time will realize that the inadequate film no longer has a market and a radical change will take place in the Mecca of the movies, and the other countries will follow its example and for the first time the example will be good since it is the American cinematographic industry that actually set the pace for world movies.

Can the cinema help the peoples discover themselves, know themselves better and appreciate one another? There is a fine theme offered to the amateurs of discourse who turn irresistibly to the more common and optimistic places. Certainly it should be possible, but motion picture production is organized and controlled in such a way that it represents hardly anything concrete.

The screen can truly depict the people of each nation and in turn, each region can feature its traditions, civilizations and cultures veraciously. We should not forget that the cinema is the least free of all media of communication that exist in the world; hemmed in by two equally negative censorships. One; the censorship of the industry itself; the other national, controlling the distribution of national as well as foreign films. The former prohibits showing any film that borders on the controversial; the later prohibits the movie-goer from seeing foreign films which have not been censored.

Thus, films of one nation are censored by another. The pattern is: learn what the Government authorities allow one to show. The condition is that the thoughts be completely uniform and in accordance with what the Government authorizes.

In spite of all this, the cinema still has the opportunity to bring people together through a better understanding of social, intellectual or religious traditions.

The fiction films and documentaries are also subjected to the same regimentation. Let us examine closely how the fiction films at present follow the same course as the documentaries. There is now a greater tendency of placing the action of feature films in areas that in the past were reserved as subject matter for documentaries, factories, farms, mines, etc. More and more producers are forced to choose themes and personalities in the contemporary scene that in the past inspired them to make documentaries; the problem of labor, of psychology, etc. They have tended to free themselves from the study of all that is artificial and to use authentic people and places. This technique and this tendency evidently have their disadvantages. Thus the problem serving as background for a fiction film cannot be subject to a study as profound as in a documentary that deals with the actual problem. On the contrary, the influence of feature films is infinitely superior notably because this type of film commands a larger audience. This is a more constructive viewpoint which producers should follow and turn away from the banal themes, thereby concentrating on deeper and more controversial topics.

Producers and directors above all should learn from contemporary life and should know intimately their country and its people—their joys, sorrows and the problems of their daily life, in order to recreate them on the screen.

If the cinema industries of all countries, in a common effort based on logic and adaptability made an effort to bring to the screen a realistic picture of their people, then we could truly say that the need for censorship could be decreased.

Censorship stifles works that do not have a conventional motif and an apprehension about the censorship paralyzes the more daring and unconventional films. What impression could the films made in Paris during the past ten years possibly give the English-speaking countries? Should they judge France by the films of the past decade, what reactions would they have? That the large cafés have terraces that practically invade the sidewalk, that people dance in the streets, that marriage is a farce, that free-love and adultery are glorified. But have they revealed the true French character and spirit?

A conscientious censor denied Claude Autant-Lara, director of *Devil in the Flesh*—and André Cayatte, Director of *Justice is Done*, the right to film the case of the unfortunate Breton, *Seznac*, who served twenty years in prison for a murder he did not commit. The obstacles were so insurmountable that the project was dropped since the censor would not approve a film that featured a miscarriage of justice. Needless to say, the authorities realized that to bring this incident to the screen would produce an unfortunate reaction. Producers may find inspiration in themes of religion, liberty, love, life, death or money but they must exercise caution to insure that their work will be accepted by the ever-watchful board of censors.

Therefore, what worthwhile ideas can the films expound for the foreign market if they can deal only with banal themes? The general impression of French films is an "Eat, Drink and be Merry, for Tomorrow we may Die" attitude, or as the French say "Vive Madame La Marquise." The preoccupation of the theatre with pictures of this sort gives the impression that all is well with the world. A film of this type tends to create an erroneous impression of life and gives rise to a false sense of well-being. Though revealing little of the real and profound life of the nation, French producers at least contributed to the rapprochement of the people through their work and brought about a measure of reconciliation with the enemy. For example the film *Le Grande Illusion* brought a German and a Frenchman face to face without hatred at a time when historical events had made them seemingly irreconcilable enemies.

Evidently the film was banned in Germany even though the director had the best of intentions. The Germans were apprehensive that the picture would backfire. They feared possible disturbances that might be inspired directly or indirectly by the film. This picture was exhibited to the public over the most vehement protests since the painful wounds of the First World War were still so deep in the hearts of the French that they could not easily be forgotten simply by looking at a film, although of excellent quality, as Charles Spaak, President of the French Motion Picture Guild, observed.

Clearly, a reconciliation between Germany and France to the end that they may live together in peace is a very important matter, but it will not be attained through films that promote this reconciliation by assuming a supposed superiority of one people over the other, no matter how good their basic intentions may be.

And also, we must consider the reactions of those attending the cinema who for example, might have been prisoners of war in a Nazi concentration camp and will experience deep emotions upon seeing recreated before their eyes experiences of bitter memory.

Although Mr. Spaak may feel that the motion picture may suffer from this type of censorship, the fact remains that the little good that this type of film may do cannot balance the disturbed impressions of the audience. Mr. Spaak's UNESCO publication comments that films which are too nationalistic in character are detrimental to world understanding.

We are in accord with Mr. Spaak on several points, especially that which refers to censorship that often will change the mood and intent of the producer of a given film, transforming a fine work into a commercial vehicle. Nevertheless, if censorship did not exist, the danger would be greater, since producers, without scruples and ambitious for money, would produce only films of suspense and sexual obscenity which are saleable throughout the world. This abuse of the cinema may directly or indirectly provoke great disturbances in the individual.

As we can see, it is a vicious circle. Only a truly profound and sincere collaboration with the producer who possesses high moral principles can improve the quality of the films exhibited to the public.

Complete freedom of expression should exist under a democracy. The cinema is the most expressive medium of all but without sane and just controls, it involuntarily can harm many people.

VIII YOUTH AND THE MOVIES

Indian film: SONG OF THE ROAD *(Pather Panchali)*
Uma Das Gupta
Directed by Satyajit Ray

Japanese film: RASHOMON *(Rasho-Mon)*
Toshiro Mifune, Machiko Kyo, and Masayuki Mori
Directed by Akira Kurosawa

Franco-Italian film: WOMEN WITHOUT A NAME *(Les Femmes sans Nom)*
Valentina Cortese
Directed by Geza Radvanyi

Mexican film: THE VAGABOND *(Vagabundo)*
Leticia Palma
Directed by Miguel Marayta

German sex-education film: TOMORROW I WILL BE A WOMAN
(*Vom Mädchen Zur Frau*)

French film on which author collaborated: THE LADY FROM MAXIM'S
Saturnin Fabre, Jacques Morel, Arlette Poirier, and Robert Vattier
Directed by Marcel Aboulker

Duel: SCARAMOUCHE
Stewart Granger

Close-Up (American Plan): THE LOST WEEKEND
Ray Milland and Jane Wyman

Chapter 8

YOUTH AND THE MOVIES

There are countless adults today who complain about the amount of influence which movies have in the life of children. For good or bad, whether they are dangerous or beneficial, the movies exist. At the very least they represent a factor in daily life. No one can deny their importance not only to adults but also for children.

An investigation made a few years ago in Great Britain by Mrs. Henrietta Bower and taken from a book by Henri Storck entitled *Le Film Recréatif pour les Spectateurs Juveniles*, published by UNESCO, makes the following assertion: Out of a total of seven million children in The United Kingdom aged from five to fifteen years, 1,250,000 go to the movies at least twice a week; 550,000 at least three times. For the latter group this means a total of 1,500 movie sessions in ten years, without counting the showing of adult films put on in the schools. From these statements it may be concluded that the cinema today contributes to the molding of the child. If it contributes toward giving adults certain conceptions of the world, its influence is even more profound when it operates on more pliable individuals, particularly sensitive to emotions, vulnerable to psychological shocks and who, precisely because they have these traits, are incapable of judging its importance. However, it would be an exaggeration to claim that only the movies provide emotional shocks for children. Life often undertakes to use other means for forming an image of the world, assisted by books and newspapers. We can better judge the influence of motion pictures, than we can newspapers and magazines. Furthermore it is possible to select films for adults, although children may see them, often even accompanied by their parents.

Westerns, gangster films, films of adventure or romance, filmed in life or in animated form, all unfold before their eyes with a certain hypnotic power emanating from the lighted screen, which holds their attention. The production of films for children presents all sorts of problems.

An international committee has undertaken to make juvenile films, a fact which is attracting the interest of various countries. At present, this effort on the part of the international committee has succeeded only in producing very little for world-wide distribution.

Other suggestions are being studied for a final solution of the very delicate problem. Clubs and societies, realizing this difficulty, are already organizing movie showings for children, choosing those films which are the least objectionable and the most adaptable, a task which is not always easy.

It is common in certain circles to attribute to the motion picture industry all kinds of failings, to blame it for errors and even for the crimes which children commit. Some people assert that its influence leads at least to immorality, if not to delinquency. Its erotic boldness, sometimes timid and confined to kissing, gravely disturbs the young viewer. Are they right? In certain circumstances, they surely are.

We are in the habit of judging the influence of movies on children by influence they exert on us. According to Dr. Le Moal, the influence on children is entirely different from that on the adult. He himself conducted an important study in France with reference to children from the age of five years to puberty. The problems of sex and amorous complications create in the children only a profound indifference and a certain amount of boredom. We do not agree completely with Dr. Le Moal's point of view, because the reaction is much stronger than he indicates. Boys and girls over 15 years of age prefer films of romance and adventure, including western and historical films. To accuse the cinema of contributing to the delinquency of minors is not always fair. In most instances the first step toward delinquency is psychological maladjustment, a familiar condition of nervousness, a feeling of ineffectiveness or insecurity.

It is not probable that a gangster film will lead into crime a boy who, on leaving a movie, has a home life which is united, happy, and prosperous. But if he lives in a slum or in the street, and if he sees his drunken parents fighting every night, he will not need the movies to teach him crime. This is not to deny that this element is more susceptible to any sort of escape, as the judicial statistics on minors show us. On the other hand, the child from a wealthy environment tends more toward all types of theft, vagabondage, questionable places, which in many instances some films suggest to him. All in all, motion pictures present very pressing and serious problems, since a trace of emotional shock may remain with us for life.

A number of studies conducted on this problem have led to very different conclusions. Thus, R. Ford, in his book *Children and the Cinema* cites an investigation made in conjunction with the directors of British film clubs, which made possible for him to prepare a list of the most frightening subjects, with scenes of mystery, crimes and brawls. After an experiment conducted by Mrs. Bower, a child was questioned and she regarded this as a typical response: "I like mystery films because I never know what may happen." Mrs. Bower declares that the child says nothing to indicate that these scenes frighten him because he enjoys experiencing fear.

Let us take another study made by Armand Lanoux, a French writer and expert on juvenile films. Mr. Lanoux feels that *Pinocchio, Snow White and The Seven Dwarfs, Bambi* and *The Thief of Bagdad* are four films which can cause violent shock and intense emotion in children. "In *Snow White* it is the metamorphosis of a fairy into a witch that impresses them most; in *Thief of Bagdad* all the children are frightened by the nightmare fight with a spider and in *Bambi* the fire in the forest is a shocking scene for young minds. In *Pinocchio* the sequence where the bad boys begin to change into donkeys is of genuine nightmare quality."

Moreover, it should be noted that the colors of animated cartoons produce a violent excitement in children which is fundamentally different from pleasure, especially in Technicolor as in American films. In his excellent work *Sociology of the Film*, edited in England, J. P. Mayer concluded that often there are films which impress children so much as to obsess them and cause nightmares and insomnia.

Many children are victims of emotional shocks from seeing adult films, some of which even have caused psychological traumas. On the other hand, Dr. Elliott Jach says that horror scenes are beneficial in that they permit children to free themselves of the anxieties and innate impulses which they constantly repress.

We do not want to launch here a discussion of the nature and esthetic virtues of motion pictures, but nevertheless, it is wise for the sake of justice to say that this is an art or a diversion which should demand of the viewer only the most fleeting feelings and in which emotion should not be solicited. Motion pictures are today the source of innumerable objections, where the good gains nothing in comparison with the evil, which almost always wins out. On the other hand, motion pictures present, in most instances, a false image of the world and of life. In the Pelican book *Film* (London 1946) Roger Manvell gives a list of cliches in Anglo-Saxon pictures, such as:

a) Luxury, especially for women, is normal.

b) Men are sources of money for women.

c) The sex problem is the most important of life.

d) The foreigner is regarded as a mistrusted person; the Oriental as a parasite.

The films which present this information are open to children. At the end of his book the author concludes that these failings are apparent not only in Anglo-Saxon movies. In this respect, the fault seems to be general.

Let us return to the last point in this list; the image of the foreigner which movies suggest to many children is the only one they will retain for a long time. It can be a source of many misunderstandings which at a future time can cause serious consequences. Of course there are exceptions.

All who saw the film *La Dernière Chance* (The Last Chance), a French production—children and adults—retained a memory which will permit them to understand better the problems that passions create. In this film, no matter what language one speaks, each person is just a human being.

Custom, which under the circumstances the motion picture industry must respect, expects that the conclusions drawn from the reports, *Children's Entertainment Films*, indicate that for children's entertainment, characters who play villainous roles should be clothed in the conventional symbols of evil, dress and ornaments, without being repulsive or frightening.

Mr. Henri Storck wrote in his publication for UNESCO, *Le Film Recréatif pour les Spectateurs Juveniles*:

"We observe that the feature which is characteristic of the occidental spirit of today is to equate the bad with the poor. In the period of the melodrama, the villain was represented by a noble, a cruel and powerful individual."

The least reflection reveals what danger to society is contained in this identification of the "bad with the poor" which the movies suggest.

In presenting to children images of a world which they do not recognize, the movies run the risk of suggesting to the children dangerous feelings of superiority or inferiority, which is no less harmful.

Such is the customary nature of the cinema, in danger of becoming still more inflexible, and caught in the chains of a society which defends and respects it.

To attempt to change the movies and make something different would be a senseless project. There is no human progress which does not aim to improve human conditions, instruct men and bring them nearer to one another, although sometimes worsening their lot and making them hate one another. Since this is the case, it would serve no useful purpose to call attention to those who are directing the evolution of the cinema, since this would perhaps entail serious consequences. Whether those who produce films like it or not, the movies constitute a new element of culture. And yet, in their progress, it is necessary that they do not forget that culture exists and that producers form a part of it.

IX THE FILM INDUSTRY DEFENDS ITSELF

A) *AMERICAN*

B) *BRITISH*

C) *ITALIAN*

D) *FILMS ON ART*

Chapter 9

THE FILM INDUSTRY
DEFENDS ITSELF

IX A) *AMERICAN*

It is fashionable these days, especially among the more vocal critics, to overlook the moral and intellectual qualities of American movies.

Instead, sharp criticism is levelled against pictures that give a false representation of Present American life. Both within the United States and abroad critics refuse to see the American cinema more than mere glorification of money, sex, Cinderellaism, female adventurers, gangsters, opulent show and romanticism, as though all American cultural life were limited to these subjects.

"These objections were not always without basis," observed Bosley Crowther, motion picture critic of *The New York Times* "and there was a time when American movies gave a doubtful image of the American Way of Life and not a very flattering concept of human nature."

Abuse of sensationalism and gangster themes has been all too obvious, and it gave rise, mostly among the narrow minded and badly informed, to a false and insulting picture of American civilization that still persists in certain circles and has yet to be effaced.

Even today American movies can scarcely be considered above criticism nor can they be regarded as the ideal vehicle for the dissemination of wisdom and inspiration to minds and consciences throughout the world.

Hollywood still turns out trashy films, follows stereotyped patters and exploits lush themes in which human nature is deceptively cloaked in flashing romance. Since virtually all American films are exported, it is to be regretted that those of poor quality are still in the majority.

In January 1960, the Oxford University Union in Oxford, England, staged a large-scale debate on the issue, "That this House holds America responsible for spreading vulgarity in Western society." American-made motion pictures, and television films, were assigned most of the blame. And during the same week, C. A. Lejeune of *The Observer*, one of Britain's most serious and respected film critics, suggested that most Hollywood films present America as a country where "marriage is simply a prelude for divorce," where "education is a synonym for necking" (contributing to a high pregnancy rate among schoolgirls) and where "the great national institution for both male and female" is drinking.

These comments are typical of the European reaction to American films, not only at present but for many years in the past. Unfortunately, the situation may be expected to get worse before it gets better. With its new-found freedom subsequent to the relaxing of code tabus, and its all-out drive for "adult" fare Hollywood has currently been indulging in a long series of films that have been outspoken both in their language and in their themes. Hollywood has, so far at least, limited most of this cultural expansion to sexual themes. Sex has always played a dominant part in the appeal and the *advertising* of the American motion picture; the only difference is that *now* the films are delivering what they promise. This is an unfortunate circumstance only in that it is being overdone and film after film, whether it be comedy, western, horror film or straight drama, has been bringing in the most explicitly stated overtones of sex—rape, seduction, pregnancy out of wedlock, perversion and so forth. Right now Hollywood is particularly vulnerable to the kind of attacks that have always been its lot, and the current "adult" cycle has been provoking those attacks on its home ground—from columnists like Hedda Hopper, from producers (albeit those who specialize primarily in *non*-adult films!) and from independent producers.

However, it should not be forgotten that the world sees far more of Hollywood's output—as a whole—than it does the product of any other country. The sexual content of many French, Italian, German films far exceeds in specifics, that of even the most blatantly erotic U. S. film. (To meet this competition, many of the Hollywood studios have been shooting additional footage for European markets: scenes of sex, violence and nudity, often involving surprisingly prominent stars, that do not appear in the United States domestic versions. Thus, criticism from abroad is often based on material in films which never pretended to reflect U. S. tastes, and was deliberately doctored for European tastes!) The same criticisms levelled against U S.. products could, and possibly would, be levelled against the products of other countries if enough of it was seen outside of its native country. We tend to use Italy's *The Bicycle Thief* as the yardstick for measuring Italian films—yet it was not popular there, and was considered an *un*-typical film by the Italians. The stream of violence-charged melodramas turned out by their studios are relatively little shown here. Similarly, we are inclined to judge *Rashomon* as being a sort of symbol of Japanese films. Yet in its own country it was regarded as an artificial and pretentious "arty" film, designed to appeal to export tastes.

Hollywood is vulnerable largely because almost all of its product is shown throughout the world and because foreign critics, unaware of the economics of the Hollywood industry, tend to evaluate all films by a rigid set of standards. They find in *The Wild One* undeniable artistry and merit; and they look for the same merits and nuances in *High School Confidential* and *Girls' Town*. When they don't find them, they turn their attention to the "neurotic society" that the films allegedly reflect. Forgotten or overlooked is the fact that these commercial films, unlike a serious (if irresponsible) film such as *The Wild One*, are produced only for the teen-age market—which is a big, and commercially all-important market in the United States. *High School Confidential* may piously claim in its advertising to be an important social document, but actually it's following the old game of playing both ends against the middle—exploiting teen-age hooliganism all it can, but dressing it up so that actually the teen-age delinquent finds himself more extolled than condemned, regardless of sex, savagery, and drug addiction. There is no denying that America *has* a serious delinquency problem, and there is no reason why that problem should not be dealt with intelligently on the screen. *The Wild One* did. So did *The Blackboard Jungle*. But the streams of quickies like *Girls' Town* and *Drag Strip Riot* have no such sincere motives, and though drawing their material from a certain aspect of American life, they are nevertheless as withdrawn from contemporary reality as the old-time western—or the Flash Gordon interplanetary adventure. Both of those schools remain on the *fringe* of reality—the western echoing the past, the science-fiction looking into the future. So does the average teen-age exposé remain on the fringe of contemporary reality—but far more dangerously so, since its fantastic exaggeration is not apparent to the overseas viewer. Without doubt the average film of this type is a cultural and artistic affront, and in these days especially its export is politically and diplomatically tactless, to say the least. Economically however, they are good bets—and indirectly they bring in the money which helps to balance off the losses on worthwhile films which fail to make a profit.

Hollywood's main problem is that in these financially precarious days, it cannot afford to make *serious* social films. To attack teenage moral standards would be to alienate one of its biggest markets. To venture into the international political arena would be dangerous in view of fluctuating State Department policy. There are still many (literally) red faces in Hollywood thanks to the film colony's wartime romance with Russia. *Mission to Moscow, North Star, Song of Russia,* and *Days of Glory* are all pro-Russian films that Hollywood would like to forget. Writers and directors, mindful of earlier events, are understandably reluctant to try anything off-beat in a political vein because of future potential black-lists. All of which is a great pity, for Hollywood is currently saying nothing of importance in a social sense at a time when there is so much to be said. Glance back at the late twenties and the thirties, when the big issue was the depression, the gangsters and wholesale unemployment. Such grim themes did not necessarily make for popular entertainment—especially with audiences wanting and needing escapism above all else. But such themes were tackled, courageously and honestly, in films like *I am a Fugitive from a Chain Gang, The Public Enemy, Heroes for Sale, Our Daily Bread* and even in the musicals— *Hallelujah, I'm a Bum, Goldiggers of 1933* and *42nd Street.* The difference was: nobody could argue with the celluloid crusade. There was no doubt that reforms *were* needed, and no important segment of the box-office public would be alienated. True, this did not make them box-office, and thus their very production is a matter to be applauded; but they were relatively free of the potential repercussions that could afflict "message" pictures dealing with today's problems.

It's a sad but true fact that the proportion of good pictures made has descreased in direct proportion to the rise of production costs, and the added burdens of increased "supervision" from the banks and increased interference from pressure groups.

In a purely aesthetic sense, no period of the movies produced as many *great* motion pictures as the silent era. The great masterpieces of D. W. Griffith—*The Birth of a Nation, Intolerance, Broken Blossoms, Isn't Life Wonderful,* King Vidor's *The Crowd,* Brenon's *A Kiss for Cinderella,* Murnau's

*Sunrise, Greed, The Big Parade, White Shadows in the South
Seas.* The work of Chaplin, Mary Pickford, Keaton, The
Gishes, Greta Garbo; the wonderfully zestful entertainment
provided by the films of Douglas Fairbanks Sr., Harold Lloyd
and Rudolph Valentino, and the richly moving performances
of The Barrymores and Chaney. This was the movies' richest
period. When sound came, a lot of the glory and poetry and
magic departed, never to return. But sound brought with it
a new realism that added to the impact of the social films of
the thirties and made it possible, in later years, to deal effectively with such important issues as Nazism (*Confessions of
a Nazi Spy, Hitler's Children*); anti-Semitism and racism in
other forms; (*Gentleman's Agreement, Cross-fire, Intruder in
the Dust, Broken Arrow*).

Notable films dealing with war themes (either of an individual plane, or as anti-war crusades, included *All Quiet on
the Western Front* (WWI), *Go for Broke* (Nisei-American),
The Purple Heart and *A Walk in the Sun. Mrs. Miniver, The
White Cliffs of Dover, The War Against Mrs. Hadley*, and
Since You Went Away reflected somewhat sentimentally
perhaps various aspects of the civilian's position in wartime.

Post-war problems, personal, psychological and political,
were brought out in *The Best Years of Our Lives* and *Act of
Violence. Citizen Kane* and *All the King's Men* offered sound
and often dynamic political commentary. Supplementing these
were films on the treatment of insanity (*The Snake Pit*), alcoholism (*The Lost Weekend, Smash-Up, I'll Cry Tomorrow*),
and drug addiction (*The Man with the Golden Arm*).

Of course, sound was an integral part of the creative
work of many fine craftsmen, contributing invaluably to
such outstanding American films as *It Happened One Night,
Of Mice and Men, Stagecoach, Fury, Shane* and *Limelight.*
Sound too, added lustre to the comedies—*Nothing Sacred,
20th Century, Father of the Bride*—and to the lavish musicals
and extravaganzas— Danny Kaye's *The Secret Life of Walter*

Mitty, The Jolson Story, Night and Day, The Dolly Sisters, Ziegfeld Follies, and particularly to the mammoth and quite unsurpassed musical spectacles from Warners in the early 30's, of which *Footlight Parade* is still the biggest (and loudest!) of all.

The industry is now going through a difficult phase in adjusting itself to its newly-imposed freedom (and I use the word "imposed" deliberately, for it may turn out to have more disadvantages than merits unless more self-discipline is exercised than has been observed,) and in working its way through a particularly trying financial period.

There is no lack of daring. Themes are being tackled that would seem to be non-money makers such as *The Nun's Story,* with its unusual religious theme, *Suddenly Last Summer,* with its cannabalism-perversion theme and *On the Beach* with its fatalistic approach to international atomic problems. Fantastic budgets are being allocated on the theory that only the best will bring in a commensurate box-office return. It's a strange theory, for certainly the millions expended on the new *Ben Hur* failed to make it anything but a stodgy, slow-moving, monumental bore, but a pale shadow of the grandeur of the silent version which also had its tedious moments. But it's a theory that apparently works, for the critics, whether they were deceived, dazzled, bamboozled or coerced—all raved—and the public is flocking to patronize the highly colored "games" much as Nero's populace did in ancient times! Hollywood still has the best studios in the world, the best craftsmen, and the best equipment. If it doesn't have the stars it used to have, at least it still has directors like John Ford, George Stevens, William Wyler, Frank Borzage, Fred Zinneman, William Wellman, King Vidor, Henry King, Frank Capra, Otto Preminger, Alfred Hitchcock and many others.

Hollywood's production problems are usually on a grand scale—1960 brought the first actors strike, an often feared, but never really expected phenomenon. This was another sign that the studios, large and small, had at last to accept a pressure from the actors themselves with the movies' so-called rival, television, in the middle of the dispute.

New processes—the short-lived but quite wonderful burst of 3D films (the only really new dimension brought to movies since the coming of sound), the stress on various new Wide-Screen processes—Cinerama, Cinemiracle, Cinemascope, Vistavision, Todd-AO—have constantly been devised over the past decade to provide that much needed "shot in the arm" (as industry jargon always terms it) to regain mass audience enthusiasm. These processes, allied with "bigger" pictures like *The Ten Commandments, Around the World in 80 Days, The Big Fisherman, The Bridge on the River Kwai* have also been aided and abetted by the "stunt" processes—the scents injected into the theatres for the Smell-O-Vision *Scent of Mystery, Behind the Great Wall, AromaRama;* the various gimmicks used to add shock value to horror films (the skeleton of "Emergo" in *House on Haunted Hill,* the electrical shocks coupled to *The Tingler.*) The only "shots in the arm" that really matter of course are the ones that result in more worthwhile films—in an artistic sense as well as in a showmanship sense; films that dare to tackle themes of questionable popular taste in honest and uncompromising fashion. Not many of these have succeeded; but at least films like *On the Beach* have *tried.* It is perhaps inconclusive, but nevertheless significant, that most of the more daring and intelligent films in this genre have been without mechanical wide-screen gimmicks, and often even without color. To add insult to injury, the unwary audience is forced to adhere to the newest (but yet the oldest) gimmick—"the reserved seat policy." The potential film-supporter is under pressure, by word of mouth, by newspapers, and even by radio, and above all, by *television,* to either mail in his money for tickets, or even worse, stand in line, like docile sheep to purchase tickets for the increasing and unending stream of "stupendous," "unforgettable" and "best ever" films rolled out like the Red Sea to be parted only by an avalanche of eager film-goers. By this artificial method, the movie-goers are induced to see films of such poor taste, that they normally would never think of watching, even on TV's never ending late, late, show!

Let Hollywood learn how to use its new freedom with taste and dignity, give its professionals some good scripts to work with, and then perhaps—despite the wide screen and stereophonic sound—we may again get the kind of movie-making that was both good art—and good box-office.

IX B) *BRITISH*

According to Dillys Powell, cinema critic of the *Sunday Times* of London, British films have contributed toward a reasonable understanding on the part of the public on various matters, although at first glance an observer may assert that there is nothing distinctive about a British film.

In the production *Cry the Beloved Country*, a theme with racial overtones was chosen and public interest in race relations was aroused. Directly after the war, the British industry produced a most important film entitled *Men of Two Worlds*, a story of the fight against the Tsé-Tsé fly in an African community that is torn between European knowledge and traditional native superstitions.

Unfortunately, this film was not too well received by the public and although the subject was worthy of being filmed, the vehicle was not sufficiently successful and we doubt that it made much of an impression on the public. In spite of this, we feel that the British cinema does play an important role and often contributes notably to international understanding.

In referring to *The World's Riches*, Paul Rotha demonstrated that the British people do not ignore the misery in India and the war-devastated regions of Asia. *Day Break in Udi*, another important documentary, describes the establishment of a maternity center in Nigeria, despite the opposition of local witch doctors. This release was quite notable because the film dealt not only with progress in hygiene but also with the actual way of life of the inhabitants of Udi, a simple and charming people who are anxious to preserve their ancient traditions.

The true strength of the movies lies in the ability to influence the spectator without his realizing that this is actually happening. That is the chief reason for the success of the American movies, and we believe that the British movie industry should be developed with this method in view.

But it is in making films about England itself that the English contribute most to the understanding of national and international problems. Evidently their films cannot have the Hollywood-type production. In the United States, a new nation in a state of flux, progress is natural. England on the other hand, is an old disciplined nation, with an appearance of reserve but hiding profound sentimentality.

The basis of this has been proven first by the success that the British films have had since the war, not only with European audiences but also, although to a lesser degree, with the American public. Among British films that have had a great deal of success in the United States, without a doubt the most outstanding were those that were typically British, such as *Henry V, Hamlet, Tunes of Glory, Quartet and Saturday Night and Sunday Morning*—films that made no concessions whatever to the American taste. In France, also, the British films featuring British humor are very successful. *Passport to Pimlico*, which has to do with an odd phase of international relations is a case in point. And, no less successful, was *Whisky Galore*, where the good and bad qualities of the Scottish national character were highlighted.

Romantic stories of many varied aspects such as *Kind Hearts and Coronets, Nicholas Nickleby, Johnny Frenchman, The Captive Heart*, etc. had an extraordinary success, principally in certain cities of France.

For several weeks these films were featured in Paris and everyday the theatres were packed with Parisians. The theory that a film based on national character, attracts an international public, has been definitely confirmed. The French people offer a very good illustration of this point in their reception of the British film *Brief Encounter*, which provoked a greater enthusiasm in France than in England.

The success of this film in France may be attributed particularly to René Claire, a French critic and writer. As this writer pointed out, the film was so essentially English that this in itself explained everything and there was no need for commentary or discussion about motivations or the significance of this film.

The films that make the greatest impression in foreign countries are, for the most part, those that would least be expected to do so. Who could have predicted that *The Red Shoes* would receive a prize in Japan? Foreseen or not, the success of British films today is apparent throughout the world. This type of production was begun during the war when England was badly hurt and her people were in very low spirits. Films such as *Morning Departure, The Browning Version, White Corridors* produced during this period made every effort to describe sympathetically the charm and idiosyncrasies of their uniquely British characters.

Of the "crime does not pay" genre, Hollywood-American technique was combined with British atmosphere and, with the solution to the crime, provided by Scotland Yard, a British-American production titled *Gideon's Day* in England and *Gideon of Scotland Yard* in the United States. Directed by an American, John Ford and starring British actor Jack Hawkins, it was a tasteful and well-made film, but one which did not lend itself too well to a fusion of international talents. The story of a "typical" day in the life of a Scotland Yard man, it was too restrained and British to give much scope to the romantically-inclined Ford, either visually or in content.

In America, it was considered a minor John Ford effort, and was cut down to second feature length.

Murder Without Crime was a British production played by a group of artists including the British actors, Dennis Price and Derek Farr. One does not study an actual crime because none occurs, the intended crime is suddenly and surprisingly aborted when the would-be assassin dies accidentally in a trap he himself has set.

This film is an excellent example of a merger of European technique and American know-how in a story dealing with the psychological problem of a criminal about to commit a crime; this uncommitted crime takes on an intense reality in the man's mind and he is troubled with the fear of punishment.

In spite of its merits, we do not advise that this film, *Murder Without Crime,* be viewed by adolescents or neurotic people, because the interpretive image is so forceful and compelling that it may give the spectator a real shock or inspire dangerous reactions, with unpredictable consequences.

In the last analysis, it seems to us that the opinion of Dillys Powell is correct, when she asserts that "people have analogous tastes and the most important thing is to offer an authentic interpretation of human nature, as it actually exists in the different countries." She adds further:

"The time is gone when we were satisfied to show ourselves to foreign countries as a submissive nation, featuring a generation of monacled dukes."

IX C) *ITALIAN*

According to Luigi Chiarini, Director of the weekly magazine, *Bianco e Nero* specializing in cinematographic research, three requisite factors for good international understanding are inherent in the cinema: its widespread popularity, its visual and concrete nature which makes the cinema such a marvelous instrument for the transmission of knowledge, and its artistic character. In dealing with an individual, a theme of universal application can be illustrated. This explains why we would like the cinema to stress educational, cultural, and scientific productions. Since the cinema can be an artistic spectacle, even in the case of recreational films, we advocate improving the movies in order that they may not be a vulgar pastime appealing only to the baser instincts. There is also the danger that they may become a malignant influence poisoning the minds of the public as an instrument of ideological and political dogmas that respect neither human dignity nor the good critical sense of the spectator.

Taking this as a point of departure, we should appreciate the services rendered by the Italian cinema to the cause of international understanding in this confused post-war world and acclaim the vigor with which Italian films affirm and defend essential human values; for without the human element it is not possible for the cinema to grow in scope.

Art is an abstract form neither moral nor immoral. Its educational value cannot be questioned and the objective is to give the public an artistic work that really speaks an universal language.

The success of post-war Italian films throughout the world was due to the fact that, answering to purely artistic demands, they filled the need to express strong emotional sentiments resulting from the cruel experiences of the war. They tell us of the shattered or forgotten human values, combat violence, injustice and misery and reawaken respect for the individual. That is the reason why these films, whatever may be the political inclination of the screen writer; are penetrated with an authentic Christian spirit.

It would seem at first glance that for producers art is not an essential factor. They seem to look for a form of immediate and clear expression with no attention to perfection of technique. Their only desire is to express clearly what they have to say.

For example, the film *Open City* by Rossellini describes an episode of life in the Italian capital under German occupation, depicting highly individualized characters, individualistic even in their manner of speech. The film won success all over Europe because in every Roman, the spectator whatever his nationality, discovered a man with his own passions, sentiments and suffering, the human victim of brutality; blinded by war but, far from considering himself defeated and resigned, continuing the fight until the time came for him to make a sacrifice for a better world in which man will no longer act like a wild beast toward his neighbor.

The film *Paisan* by the same director—Rossellini—also presents different types of regional Italians from Sicily to the swamps of Comachio, with their blunt frankness, their misery, their heroism, and their religious faith, during the period of upheaval when the Allied troops were advancing northward. The film portrays the painful effort of a people, and at the same time of all peoples that experienced the war.

Other films; principally Luchino Visconti's *The Earth Trembles* (A Terra Trema) and *Obsession* (Ossessione); Giuseppe de Santis' *Bitter Rice* (Rizo Amaro) and Pietro Germi's *The Path to Hope* (Il Camino della Speranza) show in all their cruel reality certain touching aspects of Italian life and from those scenes there arises spontaneously and without undue rhetoric an aspiration for greater social justice. The problem is particularly acute in present-day Italy, where economic inequality is more apparent than in other places, but it is not exclusively an Italian problem since the situation exists in every country to some degree. In the films made by De Sica and Zavattini, *Shoe Shine* (Sciuscia), *The Bicycle Thief* (Ladri di Biciclette) and *Miracle in Milan* (Miracolo a Milano) the social problem is individualized through the hero and the characters in the story.

The renewed vindication of the rights of the individual is of deep concern to the masses. The neo-realism of these two authors is ideological but impregnated with warm human understanding.

We could say that this neo-realism is more concrete because behind the stereotypes that represent people and social categories, we discern the real thing: the human integrity, the man who feels, believes, thinks, acts,—indeed our counterpart.

Films like *The Difficult Years* (Anni Dificili), by Luigi Zampa, *The Sun Rises Again* (Il Sole Sorge Ancora) by Aldo Vergano, *Umberto D* and *Bread, Love and Dreams*, (Pane, Amore e Fantasia) by Luigi Comencini, *Villa Borghese*—a Franco-Italian production—by Gianni Franciolini, *Clothe the Naked* (Vestire Gli Ignudi) (Vêtir Ceux Qui Sont Nus), yet another Franco-Italian production, by Marcello Pagliero, *Under the Sun of Rome* (Sotto il sole di Roma) by Renato Castellani and *One Day in Our Life* (Un Giorno Nella Vita) by Alessandro Blasetti, are indeed outstanding, and although they are reduced at times to a complete simplicity, contribute to make better known the Italian people as they are today and express humanely in an artistic format, the universal aspiration for a social justice that will take into account the rights of the human being. Such films are the expression of a new humanism. They try to convey to men a true comprehension of reality, "Such in my opinion" says the already cited Luigi Chiarini, "is the great service that the Italian cinema renders to the cause of international understanding."

In addition to this, the cinema becomes a means through which men see an immediate reflection of all their acts and a commentary on their responsibilities in life. As we see, it is a genre that is the exact opposite of the spectacle which we regard as an escape.

If the Italian cinema can hold to this direction it will contribute greatly toward that common knowledge which is indispensable to people if they are to understand one another, in spite of national and ideological, political and religious differences.

A lesson in art is always a lesson in humanity. Following the example of the great films, it will be necessary in the future to give more attention to the development of documentary films of high artistic scientific or cultural caliber.

To quote Zavattini, the prominent Italian writer:

"These films may furnish an excellent means with which to show people in foreign countries all about our traditions, our people, our national characteristics,—in fact, our soul."

IX D) *FILMS ON ART*

When an actor completes a short film that has as its subject plastic art or a group of plastic art works, he receives the congratulations or censure of specialized critics who generally are his colleagues and he may even receive a prize. But what happens to the film?

This creative collaboration of the cinema and the plastic arts did not come about only yesterday. Some of the early art film work was by Henri Storck, Belgian director-producer-writer—who in 1935, produced *Isle de Paques*, describing the population and culture of Easter Island. Mr. Storck directed and edited *Le Monde de Paul Delvaux* (1946) on the life and work of the famous Belgian surrealist painter; *Rubens* (1947) on the Flemish artist's life and work: and *Open Window* (1952) in color based on the paintings of the Middle Ages to French impressionism. Charles Dèkeukelerie, Belgian director inspired by the films of Henri Storck, produced *"Thèmes d'Inspiration"* (1938) a comparison of figures and landscapes in old Flemish paintings. Curt Oertel's film *Michelangelo* (1940) and André Couvin's films, *Agneau Mystique* (Mystic Lamb) 1939 based on Van Eyck's life and work and the treasures of the Ghent Cathedral and *Guernica* (1950) based on the work of Picasso, were all elucidating films. Alain Resnais of France directed *Van Gogh* (1948) describing the life and work of the tragic Dutch painter.

Indisputable works of art have been completed and their

authors believe that the profession is so old that they fear the result of numerous clichés.

They work hard with a professional competence and a desire for the creation of a "commercial cinema of quality not seen for many years."

L'Art Plastique of Brussels printed a UNESCO catalog in three parts: *Film on Art* (1949), *Film on Art* (1950) published in 1951, and *Film on Art* (1953). This three-part catalog was distributed to eighty-one member nations of UNESCO.

In theatres showing specialized movies around the world the documentary has its opportunity as well as the scientific short films. The film on art, on the other hand, seems banned by the theatre owners who, undoubtedly, have decided that the public is not interested in art and insist on showing the sensational and "run of the mill" films. The few experiments completed by Henri Storck of Belgium, Luciano Emmer of Italy and Alain Resnais of France, are now forgotten in the deposit vaults. Their films could show the most uninformed people many aspects of the world of painting, architecture and sculpture. They could make the most uneducated people understand the noble quality of a Van Gogh, or a Picasso; they could convince them of the artistry in the Franciscan masterpiece of a Giotto or a Fra Angélico . . . as George Fradier has said: "This could revolutionize the present trend and it is an aim for the future."

In 1950, Robert Flaherty presented *The Titan,* based on the life of Michelangelo, which received international recognition. In 1954, Twentieth Century Fox produced a series of art shorts on Botticelli, Degas, Vermeer, Renoir, Raphael, and others, filmed in such renowned galleries as The Louvre, the Prado, and the Borghese Gardens. The films were successes artistically but failures financially.

In 1956, Clouzot, the celebrated French director—produced a feature film *The Mystery of Picasso* where he depicted a living artist, Pablo Picasso, showing his style, his inspiration, and his personality.

Some short art films were made in France, taking the camera into the homes and studios of such distinguished painters as Henri Matisse, Pablo Picasso, Maillot, etc. All were made in the post-war period. Other films were based on the paintings of Vincent Van Gogh and Paul Gauguin accompanied by commentaries drawn from their letters and documents. Additional films have been made in the past decade on the art of Rubens, Calder, Jackson Pollack, and Bosch.

Above all else we must educate the public and give them a good background in art for only after a great deal of perseverance and patience, can they be made to understand the value of a film on art and the worthlessness of the Western or "Tarzan" series type of film.

X CINEMA AND ITS TECHNIQUE

Chapter 10

CINEMA AND ITS TECHNIQUE

Although this sounds almost paradoxical, we can say that anyone reading a book, particularly a romantic novel, needs a good imagination, but it is not necessary to have any great psychological insight regarding the characters in the romantic novel. In the movies, on the contrary, the spectator does not need as much imagination because the images are presented to him on the screen, but he does require keen psychological perception, since facile expressions and gestures must be interpreted immediately in order not to interrupt the continuity of the story. The film script should be reconstructed by an interpretation and an approximation of images in the most natural way possible, following the chosen text.

A cultured person may not be familiar with movie material. Literary culture and movie culture are completely different branches of knowledge.

Undoubtedly general culture is valuable in commenting on and criticizing a story or the psychological approach of an actor in a film, or on the film as a whole. On a common basic level, the understanding derived from a film is not always superior to even a superficial comprehension of books that have been read. When intellectuals are distracted, unable to observe or compose themselves in the face of the thousand problems of daily life, the artist's agents who know their profession, observe every facial reaction of their client, just as a waiter will do in a restaurant, in order that he may never lose a customer who enters the establishment. The public of the same type, like a waiter or the agent, can more easily and more rapidly acquire an understanding of cinematic signals and symbols than the intellectual, who is usually less observant.

The movies as a medium of expression are still too recent for us to predict the transformation that the language of the images may bring to the progress and significance of modern culture, but it must be said that since the talking pictures, we have reverted to an old tradition that is more important in the history of humanity than written literature: the tradition of oral culture.

The film unites the advantages of oral transmission to the permanence of a book. Movies are directed to the broadest possible public, but the film itself, is not understood by everyone in the same way. To understand literature it is generally necessary to attend school and study.

Access to cinematic culture is not as simple as some may believe—just a matter of opening the eyes to understand the film. But since the motion pictures are not a passive spectacle, but require participation on the part of the audience to be understood it is necessary to develop a cinematic culture, in order that the audience may be able to interpret the films they see in a clear and precise manner.

There are several ways of learning a language and the same observation applies to the language of the cinema.

The greater part is learned by the public right in the theatre, as they see the movie before their eyes. If this definition is accepted, then clearly such study must be very superficial and inadquate.

The other method, the more profound, consists in analyzing all the angles of the movie which are seen, knowing the elements, the means, the processes of manufacture, something of the technique of the presentation of the image on the screen; understanding all the cinematographic tricks. It is not necessary to study each "travel" or moving shot one by one, taking everything apart, or every "close up" or "fadeout."

One only has to analyze one or two sequences profoundly and form a personal opinion, carefully studying cinematographic vocabulary, forming different conjectures on the images

seen; only thus will the just criticism and exact comprehension of cinematographic culture be rapidly acquired.

The film spectator should be conscious of the use of the
"insert." That is, of a more detailed pattern in which ampli-
fication is more intense than in the American stress of "two-
shots."* In an American film, as for example *The Lost Week-
End* which portrays the story of a pathological alcoholic at
the exact moment when the hero of the film "passes out" in
a delirious dream, due to the great amount of alcohol he
imbibed, there appears on the screen an image in which we
see only a blinking of the eye and a glassy stare. As with the
dialogue, the sound-track for cutting can be very helpful or
harmful and as a rule the continuity should bring the main
theme into focus. Used without coordination or as is often
the case, carelessly, it tires the eyes of the viewer and has the
same effect as an uneven painting. The sub-plots, on the other
hand, are very vague, and frequently when they are over-
used, distract the audience and we can note that in a dramatic
film the medium close ups and the full close-ups increase
at the moment when the action is strengthened and emotion
increases in proportion to the sequence of this editing pattern.
In the film *The Best Years of Our Lives*, in order to create
a real atmosphere of family surroundings, Samuel Goldwyn,
the producer of the picture, united all the efforts in order to
emphasize the value of close-ups.

In a film in which there is a duel scene, one of the two
adversaries, being wounded, falls to the ground; the next image
is a "reverse angle shot" which shows the victim's ground-
level viewpoint with his opponent above him and corresponds
to the representation of a shot when the duelist loses. The
spectator seeing this shot on the screen identifies himself in the
subconscious with either the victim or the victor and thanks

---

*A "two-shot" utilizes two people, usually a close shot, but not
a close up (head and shoulder shot).

to the technical power, the spectator participates in the screen action, placing himself in the parts of the characters, in the represented scenario.

A montage, an artistic and chronological time-lapse (and space-lapse) via dissolves or fade-outs and fade-ins are invaluable resources for provoking scenes of suspicion by expressive suggestions. Let us take for example a "B Western" in which a young woman is kidnapped by bandits and then saved at the last minute by her fiancé, the hero of the film. We can present this setting in two ways; one with the impression of great violence and the other almost with none.

1) Abducted girl (main plot)

    a) The gallop of the bandits who take her away
    b) The arrival at the ranch where she is hidden
    c) The girl is tied to a chair
    d) A witness of the kidnapping goes to warn her fiancé
    e) The fiancé mounts his horse with a scowl on his face
    f) He gallops off in quest of the bandits
    g) The saving of the young heroine by her fiancé at the very moment when the bandits were about to harm her

2) The setting in which the spectator can see simultaneously on the screen what is happening to the young woman, and what the hero of the story is doing; following always along the same line:

    a) The abduction of the girl (in principle) she should be young and attractive; this is more effective, cinematographically speaking.
    b) A witness dashes off on horseback to warn the hero
    c) The bandits take off with the girl in haste
    d)) The bandits get near the ranch (their hiding place)
    e) The fiancé mounts his horse
    f) The fiancé gallops off in the direction of the bandits

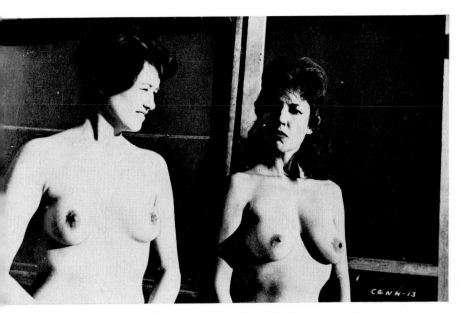

Nudist film: CAREER GIRLS ON A NAKED HOLIDAY

War film: HELL TO ETERNITY

Western film: LAWLESS COWBOYS
Whip Wilson

Tarzan film: AFRICAN TREASURE
Johnny Sheffield

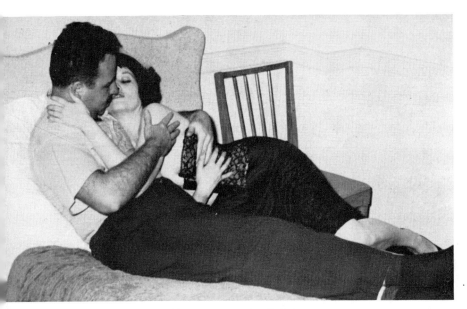

Sex film: MORALS SQUAD

Horror film: STRANGLER'S MORGUE

g) The girl is tied to a chair; one of the bandits is going to molest her (great suspense)

h) The hero arrives at the cabin with a revolver in hand, ready to shoot

i) The bandits decide to torture her to force her to talk; in the mind of the gang-leader this idea is developing and this gives some of the viewers an indirect sexual sensation

j) The fiancé violently breaks down the door and holds the bandits at bay with his revolver

k) There is a distraction and one of the bandits leaves quickly

l) The hero shoots at the bandit, wounding or killing him (in accordance with the script).

m) The sheriff arrives with his men and imprisons the bandits

n) "Happy Ending." The young girl looks for consolation in the arms of her fiancé; gives him a prolonged kiss (another sexual moment) and the film ends with a wedding.

As we can see, the second setting made with the same images as the first, is much more dramatic and gives greater emotion, and the spectator simultaneously assists the two actions that happen in two different places; they witness the girl's grief and the hero's anxiety, since they do not know whether he will arrive in time, before the girl is killed or dishonored. There is a great deal of suspense: the audience is exalted, and full of emotion following the good script of the scenarists; does the hero arrive in time or not; what will the bandits do with the young woman, etc.

Abel Gance, French producer and director, in his film *La Roue* (The Wheel) utilizes a still more dramatic editing process, an "accelerated" one in one of the scenes of these films. The engineer on a train releases the throttle of the locomotive, jumps from the train, and leaves the passengers with the risk of death.

This editing shows at the same time a scene where the train is running on one side and the passenger is shown in his compartment, on the other side. Abel Gance retakes the same images several times, utilizing each time shorter sequences and the movement is more and more rapid and more breathless; thus creating in the mind of the spectator an agony that becomes more and more vibrant and he is forced to participate involuntarily and very often subconsciously, in the impending catastrophe of the train. It can be said that during some seconds, the audience lives within the atmosphere of the accident. This type of editing creates a penetrating and sharp sensation that is also created in the mind of the audience— a feeling of anxiety, agony and suspense.

The silent movies officially vanished thirty years ago. At present all the films, even those without sound—the documentaries, for instance, are accompanied at the time of projection by music, or sub-titles. But, in spite of this, there are people who will go and see silent movies in cinema clubs. There are some art critics of the cinema who prefer the silent to the talking cinema since they consider that the former is purer and purged of today's laboratory effects but naturally tastes vary. I, certainly, prefer the talking movie, but this does not keep me from appreciating the wonderful silent films of the past. It is evident that the talking cinema has contributed to the medium of expression and this contribution has contributed to the medium of expression and this contribution has manifested itself in a screen language and in the method of presenting sequences, now in a defective manner, due to sound effects.

In a sound film, the language of the images has a predominant role, because the images are accompanied by music; the expression and mimicry of the artist is less effective. The sound also helps to direct the emotion of the spectator. A door that closes with acoustical effects, more or less noisy, depending on the circumstances; a cup that breaks; a horse gallops; the sound of a thud, trees that rustle; the wind whispers; all these are elements for the dramatic in the movies.

Words, the special noise of man, are frequently a complement of the image, and studied as such. Consequently soon the word is as necessary as the subject and enables the spectator to penetrate the secret of the soul and reveal the subtlety of the psychology of the person involved in the story that tells about the life of a common man; his thoughts, his attitudes; that a simple image, without the aid of sound, could never express.

In fact, the music that always intervenes in the film, participates also in the formation of the sentiments of the viewer; it can have a role that only with sound, links the images to the words, as well as it can present it as a sound band placed on the side of the film strip in accordance with the proper synchronization within the frame of cinematographic technique, and followed by the dialogue. The absence of external noises and of interior monologues permit the spectator to penetrate the soul of the character. During the projection of the film, the monologue intervenes at various times, as well as the commentary of the images, and reveals publicly the points of view of the characters and their internal reactions.

When we see a boxing match on the screen, or a gangster film, music is rarely useful because the images are enough to express the confusion of the moment.

When on the contrary there appears on the screen a character that seems to go back to his infancy—through the power of the flashback—the image of the man that opens the old door of the past, with a mystic sentiment, who crosses through the garden; the music helps to better express the state of the soul of this character with greater veracity than the image and the words could ever attain. It makes the spectator feel what the character feels and in this case, his own past which is relived with enthusiasm and nostalgia of a time gone by and, some times, of despair. Together with the character of the film, we will experience gratitude to the music, calm or agitation, tranquility or preoccupation. in accordance with its rhythm. The music can also give a sequence the tone that is suitable for it.

Music is developed following its own laws; at the moment in which the images need to be completed, or better understood on the screen.

The sound-track should not be neglected because at the moment when we are ready to see the images, we make an effort to hear. The sound that reaches the viewer is full of multiple significances—the dialogue, commentary to the music, the accompaniment music—in fact—all kinds of noises.

Modifying and following this, one takes vivid part in the screen's happenings or keeps silent, in order to create an adequate sound atmosphere; the fact is that this circumstance is so important that the constant change of the image on the screen may turn alive and present the cinematographic reality. An uneven sound-track can harm the good quality of the film.

The cinema clubs, growing in number every day, permit the viewer to see the films, especially the interesting ones, from a cultural point of view either old or recent productions; also such films can be shown at the private meetings, often even including scenes that the censor has cut for one reason or another. There are debates on this matter and one comes to the conclusion that the movie censor many times made a mistake by prohibiting the film.

There are also the films in general that the public cannot see except in cinema clubs. The principal interest of cinematographic sessions consists in presenting such a film and directing an intelligent discussion regarding the same.

In Italy and in France above all, before the showing of a film, a moderator will give a short explanation of the film—why it was chosen, the date it was filmed, the name of the

author, and other pertinent data. Special cultural film clubs
abound in England too and they have a high cultural level
which promotes discussions and debates among adults and
older adolescents. There they study the films from all aspects;
its aesthetics, techniques and history.

The moderator should have certain qualities as:

1) knowledge of the technique of the cinema
2) facility to speak in public and
3) the ability to begin and end and preside over a discussion

The cinema clubs in general, are opened to everyone in
order that the most diverse opinions be presented, to allow
a definite exchange of ideas on the most varied questions
possible, on the meaning of the film or on the determined
subject. The main objective of cinema clubs is to have the
spectators in a group to reflect and react on the viewed film.

Sometimes it is difficult to analyze a film by itself; an
exchange of ideas in a cinema club forces each one to remember what they saw and question one another on the impressions they got.

The viewers might learn a lot listening to other more
experienced people; in fact, it is a wonderful way to learn
the movie vocabulary and its subtleties, for the benefit of
filmology.

The viewer can see that the film is a true point of con-
tradictions between the public that is present at the show and
each one who has his own opinion for or against the film.

The artistic "formality" does not necessarily take the film
along aesthetic roads. It is easier in the movies to neglect rather
than over-estimate the creative element. To attract the spectator to the way in which the film is made, to make him
acquire a notion of cinematographic vocabulary and follow
the great progress amidst its expression: that is the purpose.

The role of the cinema critic and of the aesthetic supporters of the Seventh Art consists precisely in the facility of assimilation of all progress and technical novelties, revealing them and explaining them in detail.

The meaning of the film is important when we take in the moral question. First of all, we must combat certain conventions and preconceived notions that can foresee the judgment of a determined film. We can note that a moralizing film rarely has the value of a work of art because it loses its poetry, gaining on the other hand, the meaning of the plot. Only with difficulty do we believe in characters of a story that advances. We try to explain what compels man to act the way he does, but in depicting personalities without counterparts in real life, we reveal to the spectators characters which they can easily recognize as artificial.

Certain producers feel that we cannot believe in a movie that is powerful and humble and shows an artificial world in which evil has no place; because in life and in the profound qualities of man, there is a latent animal instinct that can be awakened at any instant, since his life is a constant struggle to earn his daily bread.

The struggle against temptation is an experience of a conventional life because the weakness of man and his misery are enormous and it is an artificial consideration that does not convince anyone. If perchance, the producers and the directors decided to show the world such as it is, without hiding it behind a wall of artificial conventions and fictitious images that exist in general, they are badly received by the public which has a certain culture and knowledge of life. The film *Brief Encounter* shows us real people who strive in an atmosphere of temptation and moral weakness and who do not give up the fight for decency and faithfulness. The film's value lies in the point of good presentation and interpretation of the close fight of good against evil, that shows the spectator moral decadence; the film ends with a superficial adjustment of the hero back in society and the climax shows the man making the right decision and carrying on his life along correct lines.

Although foreign audiences, especially the Americans, considered the solution inadequate in view of their own experiences of life, the British audiences felt satisfied by the solution due to their post-war attitude of self-sacrifice and austerity and responded to what was depicted on the screen.

As we see the grandeur of a film depends almost always on scenes with the initial artificial quality adopted and as close to the truth as possible because the public likes to remember as "delicately" as possible their own existence in this world.

The public accepts a film without bothering with the choice and indirectly is blamed for the influence of inferior films on youth's mind, since they might influence the mysterious universe of the human subconscious.

Concluding, we can say that it is the public that determines, in the last analysis, the orientation of the cinema and it is this that makes the success or failure of a movie.

The public is also responsible for the quality and production of the motion picture industry. If the orientation is at times bad, we can accuse the lovers of the Seventh Art of insufficiency of culture. By educating the people, we may expect great progress of all that which deals directly or indirectly with the scientific phenomenum conventionally known as the cinema. As some critics say, the public has been more and more "educated" in distinguishing the good films from the bad. Yet the films, according to the critics, became steadily worse for years. In my opinion these critics are wrong since "education" is not just composed of lectures and reading reviews already influenced by partiality or by simply reading in classic literature. But the "education" that I have in mind is a complete study of the subject of cinematography, as pertaining to the artistic quality of films and of the "pros" and "cons" of mass-appeal pictures and less commercial masterpieces.

Undoubtedly the best way to prevent the flood of cheap, sensational pictures is a passive one—by not attending those films. With the production of this type of movie brought to a minimum, perhaps many of the social problems of today may be lessened.

XI CINEMA AS AFFECTED BY LITERATURE, MUSIC, COLOR AND THE THEATRE ARTS

A) PRINCIPAL DIFFERENCE BETWEEN THE CINEMA AND THE THEATRE.

B) THE CINEMA IN COLOR AND ITS EFFECTIVE AIMS

C) DIFFERENCE BETWEEN THE CINEMA AND THE OTHER ARTS

D) OUTSTANDING RECENT MOTION PICTURES

Chapter 11

CINEMA AS AFFECTED BY LITERATURE, MUSIC, COLOR AND THE THEATRE ARTS

XI A) PRINCIPAL DIFFERENCE BETWEEN THE CINEMA AND THE THEATRE.

Between the romantic tendencies and the script of the film we have to a great extent many similarities, but a movie script put into theatrical form has little in common.

In the theatre, there is the famous three unit law: unit of place, of time and of action.

The first of these laws which dramatic actors rarely have transgressed—is the unit of place.

Effectively, the needs of the theatre force the author to converge in the same place—that is, to have the characters that he plans to put on the stage meet in the same place.

This rule is completely the opposite in the cinema.

One can very well create a conflict between two personages without their being in the same place. In the theatre the big theory of comedy consists of placing in a scene people who should not play together. Thus we have a comic effect.

One the other hand, we could, if we wanted to, produce an analogous situation in the cinema with a purpose that is completely opposite—that is, provoke a dramatic situation or a comic one around the fact that the personages who must meet cannot see each other.

To illustrate this example, let me mention the film:

Le Mort en Fuite (The Dead Man in Flight) with Michel Simon and Jules Berry: the dramatic situation is born the moment in which Michel Simon was condemned to death by the Jury of Paris. He was not emotionally shocked by the verdict because he knew that the assassin, played by Jules Berry, would return in time to free him.

Now, at the same time, Jules Berry had been kidnapped in Poland, taken to an imaginary country, Sergaria, where he was also imprisoned.

The dramatic situation develops from the fact that the two personages who should appear together could not meet.

We could cite innumerable examples in which conflicts are born from these unusual situations.

The unit of time, if observed in the theatre, gives a greater dramatic feeling to the action and condenses it in different ways and the classic tragedy imposes it as an absolute rule.

In the cinema, the unit of time does not exist—on the contrary—we can reinforce this action through time displacement with the flash-back. Numerous films utilize this process in conjunction with a current action, with a past action frequently increasing the dramatic interest. This process is common to the novel and the cinema.

There are numerous examples of such films, and the most descriptive were the American films, *Citizen Kane*, and *The Killers*.

The public is not absolutely conditioned to these jumps of time, in one way or the other.

The third law—unity of action—is the only rule we must respect in the cinema. A multiplicity of actions disperses the interest of the spectator.

We may have various themes in a film, but it is essential that there is always a principal dominating theme—one main idea; and that is why many films are based upon plays and novels.

From a practical point of view on the adaptation of the theatre to the cinema, there are some general principles. When a play is adapted, as it is most frequently broken into three acts, we must completely forget the theatrical form and try to find the idea contained in that which has been called the great scene. That is the center of the play or the film. The first act is really an exposition.

In "the first act" the possibilities of the cinema allow one to develop the picture and photograph different people in action and in their respective place and make them reach the moment of conflict, leading the viewer into the problems of the "second act." The third act, in the theatre is a conclusion but in the cinema it is much more concise and will suggest a possible end instead of merely emphasizing it. There we have along general lines the main principles that rule the connection of the script of a dramatic film, that is, a film that intends to tell a story to the public.

XI B) *THE CINEMA IN COLOR AND ITS EFFECTIVE AIMS*

Different tests have been made in the field of color films shown to the public. One of the first countries to see its great possibilities was the United States. We still remember *The Black Pirate* with Douglas Fairbanks, Sr. and *The King of Kings* by Cecil B. de Mille. Color on the screen is like a different world from black and white and it can be created in all elements. We do know that a certain type of descriptive cinema is not made for color—often when in color it seems to lose its dramatic value, only pointing out the need for the intimacy normally created with the use of black-and-white.

The formulas of drama or of comedy are not really the only cinema formulas. We also know that the cinema may expose and comment on the state of the soul, that is, be poetic, without having a supreme aim. In principle, the animated image should be sufficient into itself, a theme which is fully supported by the theoreticians of the "pure cinema" and the "absolute cinema."

Now, the cinematographic forms that should have an

harmonious make-up of images that are susceptible in exalting within us certain sensations or sentiments would necessarily have to be incomplete in black and white. It has the absolute need to be in color.

With the different forms, our eyes can truly analyze also the difference of colors and in their total expression make us realize that the cinema is right before us—let us say—the cinema is to our eyes what music is to our ears. The authorities also share the opinion.

For example, Mr. Louis Favre, Professor of the Institute of Psychology of Paris writes:

"We can call a colorful melody or a melody of colors, the result brought about by colors that are shown successively and the color harmony is the result produced by the colors which are shown simultaneously."

The game of colors in movement, in space, or in the precise moment does seem pleasing because it is a game. It may even be pleasing because it expresses something. "It will be easy to give colors that are immobile on the screen and the movement one may wish in relation to the emotion that one may desire to awaken. It should be easy to make numerous combinations, and these will necessarily be limited in number and truly fixed, when referring to a scene."

"The first products of music in colors, those that should appear in the future, are in a way simple. They will be simple because the present-day composers of this music will not have immediately at their disposal all the means that the composers who lived in different centuries had. They will be simple even if the present-day composers do possess all the means that a study will progressively uncover, one after the other, they could not make use of them immediately, as the public has not yet been educated along those lines."

Now the question on the part of the artists. If these artists exist, it is indispensable that they be furnished with means with which to carry out the first rehearsals. But it is necessary not to condemn color on the screen, in the theory of the principles of black and white. This has to do only with the knowledge of using an instrument that is somewhat complicated, and to carry out a difficult task for which one is not too well prepared, maybe less than more.

The admiration that we still feel for lithography or engravings is expressed in our emotion and in turn does not allow us to condemn the studies of a painter, if he does not give us masterpieces at the first attempt. Color forms, rhythms of time and of space—the cinema may be able to express all this within and outside realism.

XI C) *DIFFERENCE BETWEEN THE CINEMA AND THE OTHER ARTS*

We have had, until today, the theatrical cinema, the pictorial cinema, the musical cinema, the literary cinema, without naming other forms with less noble intentions, but now we still await the cinematographic cinema, that is, the true photogenic content, in accordance with Louis Dellux. This means that we await a poetic extreme of things or of men, susceptible in being revealed to us exclusively by the cinema. Thus we have the proposition by Jean Epstein: "I will call *photogenia* all that has the aspect of things, of beings and of souls that have a moral quality in cinematographic reproduction. All the aspects that are not enlarged by cinematographic reproduction are not photogenic and are not part of cinematographic art."

Therefore, the cinema may expose and comment on acts and gestures and there we have a descriptive form along common lines. It may also expose and comment on the status of the soul, that is, be poetic—a supreme form. Thus we go from the cine-romance to the cinematographic poem, progressing by different stages that do make use of all approaches, even if in a counter-productive manner.

As the cinema is simultaneously art of time and art of

space, this gives the image a certain plastic conception and moral revelation. Thus we have the expression: order and form. And this considerable resonance has in view the successive phases and the methods of realization.

There do exist in cinematographic composition elements that determine the proper value of each image separately, and the true value of the film in toto.

The first of these elements is represented by sentiment duly furnished in the descriptive cinema, by the subject in the scene and in the cinematographic poem, by the visual theme.

We see that sentiment is expressed and developed by itself, by the representation in which others will concur in turn; the interpretation, the staging, the clarity, the planning—in a word, that which they call, so improperly, the "mise en scène," the interior rhythm.

The second of these elements which determine the value of the image is the proper rhythm of the film, an exterior rhythm. Thus Emile Vuillermoz, the well-known French music and motion picture critic, may say that there is a real orchestration of images and of rhythms.

But it is a marvel that can become more marvelous—a 1001 times more so—even beyond the wildest dream of the cognoscenti. Whether or not this comes to pass lies not only with the love of the producer for his art, but in the last analysis, in the arms of the gods.

Did the rapid rise of the film industry come about as a result of technical innovations such as the slow motion camera, the lap dissolves, the super-imposition, montage, panning, fade-outs, and mott shots? And how much of the sudden rise was due to the coming of color and dimensional cinema?

In all primitive periods of art man fights to subjugate his raw material; inevitably the search for technique predominates. And as art develops, the means of expression change with the discovery and improvement of new techniques.

We must understand that the cinema is still in its formation. If there is still the tendency to use a technique that seems to be too similar to that of the theatre, it is because we do not yet realize that photogenic material exacts a treatment absolutely opposed to that of the theatre. Our screens are every day flowing more and more with literature for the same reason. It took a long time to divorce music and words. It will be easier to separate the words and the animated image, but we still suffer from the present incompatibility of humor.

Soon the psychology of the drama, today lasting five hours of reading, will be more profoundly felt in thirty minutes of the powerful synthesis on the screen.

While in the meantime we attempt false steps, drawbacks or fright of risk, love infected by hate, or still worse, indifference, there is nothing that is harmonious. Each is absorbed in the minuteness of detail, in the need to "fill the vacuum." I speak of the creative artists. What do D. W. Griffith, King Vidor, C. B. de Mille, Carl T. Dreyer, Victor Sjostrom, Mauritz Stiller do? What do Robert Wiene, Fritz Lang, Lupu Pick, Louis Delluc, Abel Gance, Marcel l'Herbier, Jean Epstein do?

Technique does have a direct influence on art but no art has ever used material as rich as the cinema. This material should communicate a characteristic that is very special with regard to this new work of art. The idea should try to conform to it. A face does not need in any way the same emphasis in lighting as a tapestry or a landscape. This film material is composed of thousands of objectives of which a great number are still unknown. The kind of composition that each one of them makes possible must be used.

In the cinema we have the same logic force that obliges the creator to think of images and partake of any and all developments that may be carried out in a book or on the stage. Technique has, in the long run, an indirect influence on art due to the subject presented and to the means employed and the processes of manufacture placed at the disposal of the movie director. At the present time, only one type is clearly defined; the lowest, the cinematic romance. Tomorrow its technique will be as rich as that of the cinematographic poem, but without a doubt, it will be very different, because the material will be of another quality. Thus will be the other types, especially the musical film, for which André Obey, the French musical producer, has built the foundation. In view of this extreme complexity of cinematographic technique, the general order of the evolution of the arts will be changed.

Ordinarily literature today is in the vanguard of plastic arts. This is because literature, as is frequently pointed out directly stimulates thought. There is in the arts, greater technical resistances. True, several sciences have a considerable part in the progress of the cinema. If the sculptor and the painter do not have really a great deal to learn from the little matter and utensils at their disposal, the movie director plays with material that is becoming richer and richer from day to day in modern life. To attain, penetrate, make it his own, he will have the need of very sharp senses. Real science is capable of furnishing it. Man made machine to his image, precisely to utilize forces that in another way would have escaped him. The cinema being among other things, an art of time, it captures velocity with certainty. Thought also, attains velocity without restraint. The whole world can come into the room.

According to Mr. Vuillermoz already mentioned the cinema will some day surpass literature and will occupy first place as an art form. Its means of expression will be of the richest and will have a power and rapidity that will say a thousand times better in seconds what the other arts take hours to convey—hours of reading for instance, or of contemplation.

The cinema will then receive the approval of all. Our passionate hope is that in the end it will dominate other means of mass communication but the researchers of the "original stories" may well tear their hair and may attempt in vain to hold the attention of a non-prepared public as they also might try to hold them in sentimental foolishness. This, however, will allow the art that is being perfected to make one step of progress and they in turn, will create a new beauty. The least little trick discovered by an electrician or stage technicians does more for the cinematic art than all the combinations that the romanticists may produce. It certainly will be possible to revive and evoke the past history and there is no doubt that the technique itself will impose more and more on the cinema the revelation of sentiment and of modern dreams. Scientific techniques with the advent of modern sound can be heard simultaneously in Paris, in San Francisco, in Tokyo and in the creative world. The technique creates certain orders that cannot be transgressed without impoverishing its idea and carrying it further to a literary, pictorial or musical weaknesses.

The ideal visual quality of a film may be borrowed and does not matter from whom or with what—truly, it exists in itself. We have therefore, in the harmonious presence of the images as a corolary unit, the tendency to close our eyes when we listen to music, to be tempted to put our hands over our ears in order to attain plainly the suggestions and the visual transfigurations of sentiment. Surely, we will not reach at one time such a state of grace. It would be necessary in turn, that the director follow a rhythm in his film along powerful lines and that rhythm will be enough in itself so that our view can be accommodated, exercised and perfected in the perception of infinite oscillations of rhythms. It has already been noted that if our eyes analyzed the difference of colors, forms and the degree of approximation or distance of perspective, it would not analyze the rhythmic evolution in the movement of same and would not see the movement that exists in the motion.

At the moment, it seems as though one wants above all to produce films from literary works that have already had a certain success, especially those that have acquired a kind of universal reputation. Theoretically speaking, it is absolutely indifferent that the work from where the film is taken be a literary masterpiece or pulp.

It is a point of departure. The essential thing is that the script be developed and the cinematographic rhythm be followed and that once the idea of the emotion is penetrated, it will be lent in its own "way" if not its own style; and the director will try to give it originality. In other words: an argument that served as a prime work of literature can be the basis of a terrible film, while the argument that served for a banal and melodramatic pamphlet may contain a visual idea of first rate. No matter how little it may be explored, the idea will furnish material for an excellent film. This has nothing to do therefore, with a case of adaptation of an original creation. The principal defect that could be said at present of the films of our most original directors and producers, is that the scripts are still too full of literature. The public, notwithstanding, gives its approval.

We can conceive what a creator the producer of tomorrow's great films will be and what the total reaction of profound qualities will develop. The synthesis of the whole work will attain a formidable power that some fragments of the films already make us feel.

For this work it will be necessary to have greater writers than ever before. The conception of the true producer is a fine modern poet, one that would have the necessary intelligence, imagination, sensitivity and not less, calculation and technique, regarding inaudible discoveries.

Up to date we have not yet understood that the cinema is not the only means of registering certain scenes, of illustrating a romance, a story, or even of resuscitating a theatrical piece. In the meanwhile, there is naught but a magic lantern, and if to the present moment they have not presented anything else but amateurs of clay, so much the worse for art.

Some producers will understand; but not the intellectuals, because what they look for in a film, as does the public, is the subject—first and foremost. They have a certain right, because the quality of the present films with little exception so poor that other motives of interest may be detected, or found.

Since rhythm is a necessity of the spirit, we try to find out if each one of us possesses the inate idea of cinematographic rhythm, as we possess musical and poetic rhythm. We percieve the rhythm of a wave, the rhythm of a metronome and as the instinct of imitation that makes us follow along mechanical lines the voice one hears, we are tempted to reproduce the form of the objects we see and their movements. A child will dream as long as his brain is provided with stimuli.

XI D)   *OUTSTANDING RECENT MOTION PICTURES*

IN CONCLUDING THIS BOOK we must mention such outstanding films as: the Swedish productions *Wild Strawberries* and *The Virgin Spring* by Ingmar Bergman. Among French films we should mention *Hiroshima, Mon Amour* directed by Alain Resnais, *The Truth* (La Vérité) directed by Clouzot with Brigitte Bardot and *The 400 Blows* (Le Quatre Cents Coups) winner of Cannes and Venice Film Festivals. Among other outstanding recent pictures we should mention the Polish *Ashes and Diamonds*, American—*Paths of Glory;* German—*Rosemary* and *The Bridge;* British—*Sons and Lovers* and *Room at the Top* which won Foreign Press 1st Prize Award of 1960. Among Indian pictures we should give special credit to the trilogy directed by Satyajit Ray: *Pather Panchali* (1954), *Aparajito* (1956) and *The World of Apu* (1959).

Among good pictures produced recently which also had good box office we should include: Italian—*La Dolce Vita* directed by Federico Fellini, breaking box-office records in

Europe. Others are: *Never on Sunday* (Jamais le Dimanche), *Les Amants* (The Lovers) both French. Among American pictures we have had *Guns of Navarone, Gigi, The Diary of Anne Frank, Home from the Hill, Anatomy of Murder, Elmer Gantry, The Apartment.* Among foreign pictures we can add to this category the British—*I'm Alright Jack* and two Russian pictures: *The Fate of a Man* and *The Cranes are Flying.*

We should mention also some international artistic pictures, but very poor at the box-office. They are: *The Seven Samurai* and *Ikiru* (To Live) from Japan directed by Kurosowa, who did *Rashomon,* of international fame. Polish—*Canal,* English—*Expresso Bongo,* Russian—*Ballad of a Soldier,* French—*He Who Must Die,* from Italy—*Two Women,* with Sophia Loren, *Generale Della Rovere* with De Sica. Among American films we should include in the same category: *Pollyanna,* especially for children, *The Hoodlum Priest, The Sundowners,* and *Raisin in the Sun,* and *Macario* from Mexico.

Pictures of a lower category but of big box-office among Americans are: *Exodus, Spartacus, The Defiant Ones, Psycho, Some Like it Hot, Parrish.* Among foreign: *Carry on Nurse*—plus other films which are already mentioned in the book in other chapters.

Appendix

I BRIEF SURVEY OF CURRENT BRAZILIAN FILMS

Although Brazil is as big as three-fourths of Europe and almost as large as the United States and is a nation with a population of more than sixty-five million people, its Movie Industry is not yet developed. In fact, its first step in this direction was in 1911, when one of its first films was produced. This effort, having been of a spontaneous nature and without governmental aid, did not provide continuity, and thus it can be said that the first real motion of the Movie Industry in Brazil is very recent—not even ten years old. The first notice of Brazilian movies was acquired through the films *Cangaçeiro* (The Outlaw) and *Sinhá Moça* (Missy) which were both exhibited for the first time before a big public in 1953 and which won several international prizes. Some readers might say that there were other films such as *Terra e Sempre Terra* (Land and Always Land) 1951 *Caiçara* (Beachcomber) 1950 *O Saci* (The One-legged Imp) based on Monteiro Lobato's stories for children, 1953, etc. But none of these films, with the exception of *Caiçara* were shown out of Latin America. *Caiçara* which was directed by Alberto Cavalcanti, who is very well-known on the Continent, received an honorable mention in Cannes in 1951.* Another film *O Canto do Mar* (The Song of the Sea) judged at the Cannes Festival in 1954 did not receive the critics' acclaim, which was surprising as this film was also produced and directed by Cavalcanti. This was the situation up to 1957.

The Brazilian Movie Industry is composed of two big

*I have written an article in the magazine "Carioca" of May 29, 1954 pointing out the reasons why Cavalcanti's films produced in Brazil are not as good as the ones produced in Europe—See No. 973, page 57, of this magazine.

recently constructed studios: *Vera Cruz* and *Multifilmes*. There are also compact studios, Atlantida, Kinofilmes, and Maristela, as well as smaller ones, in reality laboratories and private enterprises which from time to time produce films of average value which cannot be called regular movie productions. There are practically no cinematographic courses or schools in Brazil with the exception of a few improvised courses in Rio de Janeiro and São Paulo which are neither very popular nor of any noted prestige, for these courses only give a vague idea of the cinema and do not produce future technicians of the Seventh Art nor the future "mis-en-scène (stage) artists and directors. Hence the tremendous lack of professional artists thoroughly familiar with the movie industry. There are, of course, many amateur artists of tremendous talent—good dancers and singers, who with a good and competent director will be able from time to time, to produce an average film for the public.

A good director is rare in Brazil, but in the event that we do find one to direct a film with Brazilian artists and foreign technicians, he will have difficulty in presenting a grand opening without having the necessary group of first-class artists, of which there is a lack—not mentioning of course the lack of good sound technicians, screen adaptators and specialists in technical equipment. A handicap for the Brazilian cinema consists in the lack of financial assistance from the Government, which is common in almost all countries, but it can be well justified as the quality of the productions have been inferior to those of the average standard of the international cinema and thus the government does not want to unnecessarily spend money for something which will not give a concrete result. On our part, we think that the most pressing problem is not the financial one but the necessity of creating a group of good artists, and a more thorough understanding among men of the cinema. It is necessary to allow a certain freedom for the cinema, avoiding any monopoly which is the obstacle of all big-scale developments in favor of the people. We should consider a cultural exchange of Brazilian artists with such countries as France, the United States, Italy, etc. so that they may stay for a length of time with their studios in order to familiarize and develop within themselves the artistic "feeling" so necessary for a movie star. Also, the Brazilian Government and private enterprises should aid and attract to the country great foreign directors and technicians to produce films with the participation of local artists. I don't mean by this to say that they should attract producers of "Westerns" and "Tarzans" as these types of films do not present any artistic or cultural value but only represent sensationalism and vulgarity and which, despite their low qauility are nevertheless a very lucrative source for producer and financier, who only worry about accumulating fortunes without caring about the moral value of the film and the reactions which the spectators get in exchange for their money.

Several contests and prizes should be made popular in order to assist those individuals who are interested in the cinema art, and who want to pursue it as a career.

I will here mention several paragraphs written by the Brazilian producer, Alberto Cavalcanti, both in his book entitled *Film and Reality* and in the Italian magazine *Bianco e Nero* in 1953. Alberto Cavalcanti today is the outstanding personage in the Brazilian cinema, and this is due mostly to his foreign creations rather than to any films produced in Brazil. His prestige, however, is now being shared with Lima Barreto, the producer of the film *O Cangaceiro* which today is widely acclaimed and which was honored even in Russia and in Japan. If Lima Barreto is capable of producing another film of equal greatness as *O Cangaceiro* he will no doubt become the "man of the year."

This is what Cavalcanti tells us about the Brazilian public: "Millions are spent each day by many who want to escape for two or three hours their every-day routines, and thereby go to a movie. These individuals react in different ways to a film, but very rarely do they hate or deplore a film."

"Little matters that couples in love will take advantage of the semi-darkness of the movie house or that girls will only think of setting their hair à la Betty Grable or of living in a bathing suit such as Esther Williams. The movie public as a whole has great perception and is gifted with an extraordinary receptiveness. It accepts modern music and understands the most complicated psychological situations."

This explains something about Brazil's movie audience and in several viewpoints, I am in agreement with Cavalcanti.

Here is his opinion concerning cinema themes, also taken from his book:

"One of the most employed cinema themes, which constitutes one of the best examples of the usual cinema propaganda, is the one referring to the dissatisfied rich as well as the dissatisfied poor. These themes, repeated so often in the American films, sometimes give one the impression that in the United States the poor man would feel terrible with the idea of being a millionaire and the rich man worried with what to do with his time and, money. Also he is conscious of an ill-feeling as regards his sons and daughters who probably have been very badly brought up." Here is also what Cavalcanti says regarding the social education of the Brazilian people:

"It is a problem of great urgency not only in the interior of the country where living standards are as low as they can be, but also in the big cities, where there is a visible unbalance between social classes; and thus our first obligation and necessity is to introduce to the different ethnic groups, among them immigrants who have only recently arrived in the country, a civic sense for better understanding of our country."

And thus I end here my quote of Cavalcanti's book and his opinion concerning the Brazilian movie public. Along general lines, his observations are most accurate.

The details, however, constitute a great number of the

author's personal opinions which sometimes are not within the realm of reality. It is interesting also to cite certain paragraphs written by Alberto Cavalcanti, which were in the previously mentioned Italian movie magazine *Bianco e Nero*, entitled "Foreign Contribution to the Development of the Brazilian Cinema," in which he gives us an interesting study about this theme.

"In the early days of the Brazilian Movie Industry the carnival film, which was badly copied from the Hollywood music hall, was almost the only expression of the Brazilian cinema. It continues to be a rudimentary improvisation, of bad narration and mascaraded with the numerous Brazilian songs and dances in order to please the audience, which is most anxious to hear its mother tongue and to see their people, though they were badly interpreted on the screen. This influence is still in existence in the Brazilian cinema."

Cavalcanti says that the European cinema tries to defend itself from the Hollywood productions by producing films typical of their own countries, which American producers would have difficulty in reproducing. Thus, the English express their technical qualities, sometimes humoristic, based on solid grounds. The French films solidify poetry with burlesque love. The Italians, contrary to the French, base their films on the problems of today's Italy and try to photograph the common way of life in the country in order to relive it on the screen for the public. These last two are typical both in Mexico and in Brazil. The Movie Industry of these two countries tries to bring to the screen the exact same themes, however, within their characteristic customs.

Argentina in turn copies the Mexican farcical dramas, the Italian sensibility and the local passion of Spain."*

Cavalcanti goes on to say that at present not only the critics, but also Brazilian intellectuals understand that only a faithful reproduction of the country can give the movie industry real stability and value.

*This is not only Cavalcanti's opinion, but also my own.

Personalities, such as Professor Bardi and Francisco Matarazzo, who created the Museum of Modern Art and of Fine Arts in São Paulo which constitute a most favorable factor to the progress of Brazilian culture, also contributed to the rebirth and establishment around São Paulo of the movie industry, by giving it financial assistance.

Another interesting study is the gangster problem which was presented by Salvyano Cavalcanti de Paiva, ex-critic of the magazine *Manchette*.* In his book *O Gangster no Cinema* (The Gangster in the Cinema) he talks about the American movies and indirectly deals with the social problems and American racial problems. His book would be absolutely to the point if only the title would have been changed to *O Gangsterismo nos Estados Unidos* (Gangsterism in the United States), as he only deals with Hollywood problems, without making any comparisons with other gangster images that have existed on the screens of other countries. Besides, his work is quite partial and it is a great shame that he did not read *Defense of the American Movies* by Bosley Crowther, the motion picture critic of The New York Times, published in 1951 through the intermediary of UNESCO. If Salvyano Cavalcanti de Paiva had read and analyzed this work, he certainly would not have repeated in his book the fundamental errors of bad interpretation. For this reason the value of his work suffered a marked loss, though it is a subject of great necessity in the present day. It would be well if another expert on this matter, who is conscious of his responsibility as an author and at the same time a good propagandist of Brazilian culture, would develop this subject on a more objective basis. Doing this he will no doubt give a helping hand to the prestige of cinema literature, which is now in the phase of birth in Brazil.

It is also interesting to mention a Brazilian publication of 1952 entitled *Significação de Far-West* (The Meaning of the Far-West), written by Octavio de Faria, in which he

*"Manchette": second best magazine of Rio de Janeiro.

deals with some problems of the literature of the cinema in the years from 1928 to 1952. Here are some excerpts:

"It is true that the cinema has enriched itself with new expressions. The man with an average culture is able to understand the cinema: however, we ignore the complexity of its language. This language cannot make its revelation if we are to place it suddenly with the latest cinematographic productions." He concludes:

"Once the cinema's proper language is indispensable, why don't the directors take this opportunity to educate the audience?" We ask that if in reality the function of movie directors is to deal with this problem, or if it is the public which should refuse to accept films of inferior quality. Press campaigns and other media which would express the public opinion, could introduce cultural and social movements against the bad films, independently from the country of origin, which would produce good results. In this way one step forward would be taken, while the other step would be given by censorship, which would not allow into the country films which do not have a minimum of cultural and artistic elements, as is the case with many now shown in the country. To end this small illustration and commentary concerning Brazilian motion picture bibliography, I will mention Carlos Ortiz, author of the following books: *Argumento Cinematográfico e Sua Technica* (A Screen Play Manual and its Technique) *Cartilha do Cinema* (The ABC of the Cinema) and *O Romance do Gato Preto* (The Tale of the Black Cat—the brief history of the Seventh Art) which is a brief history of the cinema and, in my opinion, the author's best book.

The *Cartilha do Cinema* gives Brazil a certain prestige in the mastery of the cinematographic technique, and gives one an idea of the Seventh Art. In contrast, his latest book, *Argumento Cinematográfico* is very poor and deals with the complicated technique of the cinema background in a childish manner, mentioning many things without giving, however, a complete definition or solution to the problem. Here is an example which Carlos Ortiz understands as a rather banal scenery plan that of *Romeo and Juliet*. This is the segment of the script: "Romeo and Juliet glance avidly at each other. Still the sound of the sea. Still the perfume of the magnolias. Still the echo of their kisses. Romeo and Juliet's lips search each other with anxiety. They kiss passionately . . ." The text explains in itself the childishness which is the theme, terribly overworked as the screen play. We await with impatience his new work which is being prepared. It is called *Dicionario do Cinema* (Cinema Dictionary) which if it is well made, will be a source of information for the future of the Brazilian cinema and will add another important facet to the cinematographic culture of the country.

Before ending this small study of the cinematographic culture in Brazil, we should not forget the deceased Moacir Fenelon, who was the first to be thoroughly related with the re-birth of the cinema industry of the country, as well as the one to seriously attempt to create a syndicate of movie professionals. His first film was produced in 1950 by Cona-Films, *Simpatico Jeremias* (Charming Jeremias) with Darcy Casare, in which all the technical parts are under his control as at that time he could not find capable technicians. The carnival film *Tudo Azul* (Everything Is Fine) which he began in 1952 was only concluded after his untimely death.

We should also honor Antonio Leal, who can almost be considered as the Father of the Brazilian Cinema, and who on November 5, 1903 on Rio Branco Avenue, introduced the first 35 mm newsreel. He produced later on in 1916, the film *Patria e Bandeiras* (Homeland and Flags) and a few years before in 1908, another producer Paulo Benedetti produced *Uma Transformista Original* (An Original Impersonator) with Eleanor Duce and Victor Capellari.

About three years later (1919) another Producer, José Media, while in São Paulo working for Rossi-Films produced *Exemplo Regenerador* (Changing for the Best).

We should also not forget Ademar Gonzaga who produced *Barro Humano* (Human Clay) 1929 and launched almost at the same time, the first movie magazine: *Cinearte* (Movie Art) and who later founded Cinedia's studios. Thus, it is worth mentioning the films: *O Segredo do Corcunda* (The Hunchback's Secret) produced in 1925 by Alberto Travesso, *O Tesouro Perdido* (The Lost Treasure) 1929 and *Labios Sem Beijos* (Kissless Lips) in 1930 by Humberto Mauro, in which Paulo Merano, Lelita Rosa and Alfredo Rosario played the leading roles. In 1932 he produced the new version of *Ganga Bruta* (Diamond in the Rough) with Durval Bellini, Lu Murivel and Dea Selva from Cinedia. The films *Mulher* (Woman) 1931, produced in Rio de Janeiro by Octavio Gabos Mendes, *Paulo e Virginia* (Paul and Virginia) 1921 and *Vale dos Martirios* (Valley of Martyrdom) 1927, by Almeida Fleming. *Limites* (The Boundary) Mario Peixoto in 1930. The films *Alma Gentil* (Sweet Soul) 1932 *Sofrer para Gozar* (The Pleasure of Suffering) 1924, produced by João da Mata and *Mocidade Louca* (Restless Youth) in 1927 by Amilar Alves, produced by Felipe Rici and others from Campinas.

According to information acquired, the first spoken Brazilian "short" was produced in 1927 called *Ben-te-vi* made by the vitafone process. Almost at the same period Luis de Barros produced the film *Acabaram-se os Otarios* (An Easy Mark) also spoken.

In 1934 the first movie tone was produced entitled *Alo, Alo Brazil*. We shouldn't forget the films *Do Rio a São Paulo para Casar* (From Poverty to Riches) made in 1921; *Gigi* in 1925; *Fragmentos da Vida* (Fragments of Life) in 1929 *Sangue Mineiro* (The Girl from Minas) in 1929 by Humberto Mauro and *Uma Aventura aos 40* (An Adventure at Forty) 1945, under the direction of Silveiro Sampaio and others.

Of the comedy films produced after 1945, we can mention *Falta Alguem no Manicomio* (A Candidate for the Madhouse) 1946 *O Comprador de Fazendas* (The Farm Buyer) 1951

Canto da Saudade (Longing for Home) in 1951 *Simão, o Coelho* (The Rabbit called Simon) 1953 and made with the participation of Alberto Cavalcanti; *Ai vem o Barão* (Here comes the Baron) with Oscarito (a Brazilian comedian).

Sinfonia Amazonica (Tropical Symphony) 1953 by Amello Latini which took him ten years to produce thousands of animated cartoons hand-made by the author, *Tico-Tico no Fubá* (Tico-Tico) based on the life story of Zequinha de Abreu* (1952) which was shown in several countries in Europe.

Also worth mentioning are: *Gigante de Pedra* (Sleeping Giant) 1954, by Walter Khouri, a masterpiece of its kind— *Uma Pulga na Balança* (A Flea on the Scale) 1953, *Floradas na Serra* (Mountain Flowers) based on a famous novel by Dinah Silveira de Queiros and *Na Senda do Crime* (The Road to Crime) all produced by Vera Cruz Studios in 1954. *Rua Sem Sol* (The Street in the Shadow) 1954 by Alexy Viany and *Rio, 40°* (A Tropical Rio) 1955, which won special recognition at a Czechoslovakian Film Festival in Karlovy-Vary and a prize in Russia. This was quite an achievement for a production of this type.

This film caused quite a commotion in the capital of Brazil as well as in the provinces. As a result a screen censor was forced to resign. The film satirized the power of the church, the intrigues of the politicians and vividly depicted the squalid living conditions of the masses in the capital.

An important documentary was *Samba Fantastica* (Fantastic Samba) by Jean Manzon, a Frenchman residing in Brazil —this documentary obtained the 1956 Cannes Film Award.

Other films were: *O Leonora dos Sete Mares* (Oh Leonora of the Seven Seas) and *A Estrada* (The Road) by Osvaldo Sampaio, a Brazilian (1956) version of the internationally celebrated Italian film *La Strada; Sinfonia Carioca* (Carioca Symphony) winner of the 1956 Rio de Janeiro Film Festival produced by Watson Macedo.

Often at film festivals the selection of the committee is not

*One of the first pioneer's of Brazilian Folklore Music.

Censored film: FOREVER AMBER
Richard Greene and Linda Darnell

Censored film: LADY CHATTERLEY'S LOVER
Danielle Darrieux

Censored film: MARTIN LUTHER

Censored film: GARDEN OF EDEN

in agreement with that of the general public and critics, as for example with *Sinfonia Carioca.*

One of the most recent Brazilian co-productions, *Black Orpheus,* was filmed in Technicolor. It is a Franco-Brazilian-Italian production based on *Orfeu da Conceição* by Vinicius de Morais, a Brazilian poet and diplomat. The film won the Grand Prix of the Cannes Film Festival in 1959. Where the Brazilian talents, almost unknown with the exception of two athletes, Breno Mello and Adhemar da Silva, are directed by Marcel Camus and produced by Sacha Gordine and partially financed with Italian capital. It really should have been a completely Brazilian production but Vinicius de Morais, a friend of mine, could not find the necessary financial backing in Brazil and was forced to share the prestige of presenting the beauty and the atmosphere of the traditional carnival of Rio de Janeiro with the French and Italian film industry.

The *Black Orpheus* legend is based on the myth of Orpheus and Eurydice and the priority of beauty in love as adapted in Brazilian folklore. Since the whole drama is depicted in the splendid atmosphere of the Brazilian Carnival, the film in Brazil, was entitled *Orfeu do Carnaval.* Even though the film was officially registered as a French film, I feel it is my duty to call it the best *Brazilian* film since *O Cangaceiro* which also brought international recognition to the Brazilian Film Industry. Even though the French claim it as their own, it must not be forgotten that private Italian capital financed the film without which it would probably never have been made!

Homage should also be paid to the Brazilian pioneer studios, Phoenix-Films, APA Films, Phebo Films, Aurora Films, Selecta Films, etc.

With this I will end my description of the most important Brazilian films with the hope that future Brazilian films will more and more be made in accordance with international standard patterns and be satisfactory both along artistic as well as box-office lines.

II SPEECH BY THE AUTHOR
DELIVERED BEFORE THE
BRAZILIAN CONGRESS

MR. PRESIDENT, SENATORS, DEPUTIES, LADIES AND GENTLEMEN:
It is well-known that the cinema has great power along economic as well as instructive, political and educational lines, and must be efficiently organized. Our national cinema could be as great a source of wealth as coffee or rubber. Deputy Aurélio Vianna said only recently, during a speech in the Chamber of Deputies, that Brazil is now the second largest customer of American movies in South America. The greater part of imported films are from the United States since they make some 350 films a year and distribute them throughout the world.*

The President of the Motion Picture Association, Mr. Eric Johnston, stated at the annual banquet at the Hotel Waldorf Astoria that the American movie industry could not exist if it were not for the assured market outside of its country of origin.

If America, or to be more exact the United States of America, cannot be self-sufficient along those lines, then much less can be Brazil. India, which now has the second largest movie industry in the world, until a short time ago had no motion picture industry. The situation of India was very similar to that in Brazil now with regard to the motion picture industry which is the main purpose of this meeting. This Round Table discussion is very important to me and I hope it will be also for those present. I trust that after this meeting there will emerge a new era for the national cinema and that

*At present, the film production is much less; in fact, in 1959 there were only 223 films made, of which 150 were completed in this country and 73 aboard.

184

that which should have been done since 1808 will be done now. At that time the Royal Family of Portugal* sponsored the development of the nucleus of the cinema called *Camera Obscura* based on a remarkable photographic process. We are now in the Twentieth Century and more than 148 years have elapsed, if one considers that the camera was born with Lumière (this is really not factual) who was popularly called "the father of the cinema." In accordance with Sadoul, the first official cinematographic presentation to the public was made on December 28, 1895, and at that exact moment the Seventh Art was born. Prior to that it was Thomas Walgenstein who in 1798 presented his 'pahntascope," one of the first stepping-stones of the cinema. The first Niepce photographs date back to 1823, and were made much earlier. Each photograph took fourteen hours, and even in 1839 a half hour was needed. From 1851 to 1872 several experiments were made on that field, in fact, much before Lumière. An Englishman, Muybridge made the first film of a few minutes duration in San Francisco for the American millionaire, Leland Stanford.

Since 1878 in California several people tried to take photographs at random. Later in England, Friese Greene successfully projected the first films for the Academy of Science in London. We will not go into this matter any further. We only broached it to prove that the cinema has had a long existence and that in Brazil it had its beginnings almost at the same time as in other countries; taking the date of November 5, 1903, as an official date of the birth of the cinema in Brazil (this is very doubtful indeed) because Pedro Lima** believes it was much before that and we were in agreement with that observation.

Around 1891, Vita de Maio, an Italian had his "animatograph" installed in Ouvidor Street. After him came Henri

*A branch of which subsequently became the Imperial Family of Brazil.
**One of the most celebrated critics in Brazil.

Picolot, Manuel Ferraz de Campos, etc. Thus we have more than 50 years of national cinema. The American cinema was only about 15 years older. However, there exists a great difference between the American Industry and our own. Why? Not because as Muniz Vianna of the *Correio da Manhã** said that the Brazilian industry is very new and without experience. There is not a word of truth in it. The industry in the beginning in Brazil was not well organized or coordinated. The few elements that did want to do something, never received real aid. The press, instead of helping, tried to raise difficulties sabotaging the good ideas of the few visionaries who wanted to see a big cinematographic industry develop. Even top critics like Hugo Barcellos of the *Diarios de Noticias,* Alipio de Barros of *Ultima Hora,* Van Jaffa of *A Noite,* Pedro Lima of *Diarios Associados,* Ely Azerevedo of *Tribuna da Imprensa* and others, traditionally critized the national cinema in an absurd manner, very often justly but then, at times, not at all. They created a kind of antagonism against the Brazilian cinema to a point where no one wanted to see national films because they were conditioned to think that they would be bad, even without seeing them. My colleague of the *Jornal do Brasil* said quite correctly that for Alexy Viany** there is no true American cinema and for Muniz Vianna, there is no true national cinema. Both erred and the public is divided between the two trends of thought.

After completing my research work, I presented my report to His Excellency, the President of the Republic and others, in order that it could be submitted to the Congress for an opinion. This report was completed at the Vargas Foundation and considered by them as an exceptional work.

This is not a complete work, however. What the national cinema needs is an emergency plan in order that our Industry

*One of the most popular Brazilian newspapers.
**One of the more astute critics, although having marked Communistic tendencies.

may surpass in record time Argentina and even México in order to be able to face the rivalry of India, France, Italy and England. And this is a step towards progress.

Let us look at the example of Japan and Germany. Even though they lost the war, their industry has attained great progress. Each film that is exported to us deserves applause. If those two nations that are much smaller than Brazil can make good films, why can't we do the same? In 1955, in accordance with Deputy Aurélio Vianna's statements, income from movie-goers throughout the nation reached three million tickets—averaging 10 to 12 cruzeiros* per ticket. This is still not very significant when one thinks of the twelve million daily spectators who attend Hollywood productions throughout the world, as stated by Mr. Eric Johnston, President of the Motion Picture Association. The laws that were presented by Deputy Aurélio Vianna a short time ago on the dollar exchange and other convertible currencies in the market, as well as the total dubbing of foreign films in Brazil, etc. seem fine in theory.

They protect the national industry, but are we prepared to enjoy such luxury? Such a measure and other similar ones will be good in the future. Already in several other sectors of our industry, there has been considerable capital invested. Look at the magnificent growth in São Paulo and Rio de Janeiro where at present with their industry they have made themselves known to the whole world and are greatly admired in many sectors of the globe. Why can we not try this with the motion picture industry? The cinema was never a symbol of patriotism for anyone and much less so in the industrial field. It was always based on the greater possibility of making money.

That is what gave Hollywood its stupendous growth, and made it what it is today. Hollywood specialized in obtaining, no matter the cost, the best talent in the world—

*Brazilian currency.

the best stars, technicians, writers, etc. We should also do so. It is the only chance for quick development of our industry.

Only 30 years ago the American industry was still embryonic and there are analogous problems in the Brazilian situation today.

Hollywood may face a crisis. Many of the producers cannot make films in the United States. Taxes are so high that they go overseas in order to make films. This is true of the English industry also, but to a lesser degree. Taxes there are also very high. That is why stars go to México, Italy and even India to film their pictures.

Then, why not go to Brazil? We should give them the same working conditions that they have obtained in these other countries, favoring the North Americans. There should be a small but vital condition. What ever is completed in our country is Brazilian and should be incorporated into the national industry. The material transported by interested elements to our natural scenic sections for their films, in great part will remain and thus should receive better treatment on the part of the Bureau of Credit and Currency and the Bank of Brazil. The value and the importance of incorporated material will be a subject for discussion at another time. This is also applicable to other friendly nations with which we have identical commercial contacts as regards the subject referred to herein. The favoritism given to the American cinema, simply for reasons of commercial interest, can be later transferred to other nations. To obtain this, we should also make some sacrifices for the good of the national cinema. The first would be to have the same working conditions that they have in their countries and also give some special considerations that they would not have elsewhere. The essential thing is to promise them more money, greater working liberty and not to interfere in the plot of the films, if they do not harm our interests with other nations, or go against our laws. Evidently, a certain control would be necessary, as for example, a review of the plot before it is filmed. Similar to what the Motion Picture Association does, not enveloping the technical side. And that is all, with the exception of censorship on the under aged and the moral character of the film.

The artists and technicians should be chosen by the producer, if possible, among local talent. As we can well understand, the local workers are much cheaper for the producer than imported labor and being a businessman, he can understand the preferance; however, it is necessary to know if the local labor forces can do the same kind of work as their foreign colleagues.

The uncensored plot—as we mentioned—should be chosen by the producer as well as the locale for filming. In other words, the producer should have free rein in choosing topic and location. Material to be used in the film, as soon as it enters the country, becomes a part of our national industry. This does not harm the national producers who can make their films as before or with the collaboration of the other foreign film producers, if the film is not detrimental to the good name of the new national cinema. Censorship could then be taken out of the hands of the police and handled by the Ministry of Education or, better still, by a new organization— a kind of "Information Bureau," similar to that of Italy or France, or even completely different since we do not have to copy others all the time; let the others copy us.

Thus there are great possibilities, Brazil possesses great wealth, natural beauty, tourist attractions and other worthy factors. This all could make Brazil one of the foremost movie countries of the world. This new organization will have the right to censor the films in the country, as well as those of foreign origin. Many are not worthy of being shown on our screens,—especially the Tarzan, Western and thrill film groups. Many of them have no artistic quality and instead of instructing do more harm to adolescents, and even adults. The same office would be in charge of publicity and advertising of national films throughout the country and principally in foreign nations. The film in the country is very important but it is more so in foreign countries. It gives us dollar exchange and becomes an "ambassador" of our people, of our civilization, of our habits and customs. The country crosses the ocean with a well-produced film. The power of a film is very great, in fact, tremendous, "to educate for death as well as for life—it edifies, destroys or constructs. This is true especially with regard to the people who do not know our land or our people. They judge us as they see us and that is paramount. This new organization could be responsible for that and could take care of efficient collaboration among all the branches of the cinema; independent of the Government or pressure groups, as much as possible, in order that it may act as a liaison office between the different unions and to advise and represent the cinema in the national territory or even in foreign countries. That organ and its importance would grow in conjunction with our industry.

Men of prestige should be connected with it; uncorruptible individuals who will look after the movie industry as a mother does after her child.

What could be more dangerous than bad organization or internal strife among those responsible directly or indirectly for the national cinema? Harm should not come to those people connected with the national motion picture industry and indirectly the country, as it would be something contrary to the principles of the liberty of the press and the democracy in which we live. Thus, the role of the Public Relations and Information Service would be a delicate one, difficult but not impossible. It would educate and not order; even an appeal to patriotism may be used, lectures given etc., and there should be no pressures or impediments. We recommend that the small producers as well as the distributors, be independent and not suffer pressure of any kind and they should cooperate with one another.

The small exhibitors have a problem too; if they do not want to be an instrument of exploitation by large exhibitors or others who dominate the market, they should associate to form a Union and cooperate with one another through the good offices of an adequate Public Relations System. All this is easier in theory than in reality and even in practice it is difficult to obtain perfection. With an effort, we can come to a decision to satisfy the whole world, only with a difference in degree. To solve the problem that has been spoken of so often—'lack of money" a local plan can be adopted.

A Low-interest Banking Organization could be set up whereby films with exceptional qualities could obtain financial backing. I cover this matter at length in my report. They can follow the format set up by the large financial concerns by subscriptions, insurance, etc. based on a loan with guaranteed interest.

I will now speak of the International Cinema Festival being discussed so much at present. Our friends, Fernando Salgado and Joaquim Menezes*, motion picture critics, wanted to carry it out at all costs without thinking whether or not it would be advantageous to the country's economic situation. I am not against an International Cinema Festival in Rio de Janeiro or in any other place, if it is well-prepared, planned and carried out without the bureaucratic interference that did so much to hurt our first Festival in São Paulo. Instead of being a profitable venture it was a loss in different sectors; perhaps with the exception of direct contact and exchange with foreign artists. The next Festival should undoubtedly leave a profit to our industry as a fountain of resources to produce more films and not have deficit results. That should be the aim of the Mayor, the Department of Tourism, Hotel Owners, as well as of the Industry and its Public Relations and Publicity

*Long-time President of the Brazilian Motion Picture Critics Association.

Department. All possibilities of such an event should be explored and studied.

I propose that a commission be formed of competent people, composed from amongst the people present at this Round Table Discussion to study this question in detail, and present before the Congress a series of Laws to put into operation my emergency plan, and it should then be carried out.

The Commission would have to follow the laws and the projects of the Chamber of Deputies, Senate, etc. in order that bureaucracy would not penetrate into the execution of this gigantic plan—with regard to all the difficulties that it will encounter along the way before becoming law and even during its application. This commission could be incorporated jointly or separately, in all research project possibilities.

With this I terminate my speech—wholly conscious that this matter is of great importance for Brazil. I trust that my recommendations will be found helpful.

By Mark Koenigil, Graduate of the
International Institute of Filmology
University of Paris (Sorbonne) and a
Member of the Brazilian Motion Picture
Congressional Commission

III CENSORSHIP OF
MOTION PICTURES IN THE U.S.A.

The motion picture industry has two kinds of censorship: the industrial and the governmental, the latter mostly censorship by states and cities. The motion picture code grew out of threats to the industry.

After World War 1 the movie industry was caught in two social currents which were not exactly congruent. On one hand, movies befan to reflect on the moral standards of the times, notably the freer discussions of sex and family life. On the other hand, they met a tendency on the part of American people to try to correct social evils by law, one of which was prohibition. The motion picture industry faced both boycott and official censorship.

From 1918 to 1921 several voluntary organizations had scrutinized the content of the movies and declared much of it evil or worthless. Religious and civil leaders spoke against them and the daily press carried the scandalous life of the Hollywood folk. Among them was the notorious story of "Fatty" Arbuckle and, although, he was never convicted of the manslaughter with which he was charged, the story was sufficient to ruin his career and present Hollywood as a modern Babylon. People turned to law to correct the alleged abuses in the films, the same way they tried to correct the abuses of the saloon.

Between 1909 and 1922, eight states and a number of cities established legal censorship of motion pictures. Alarmed by public indignation and consequent threats of boycott the movie makers in 1922 formed the Motion Picture Producers and Distributors of America. The first resolution of this organization was to discourage the purchase of questionable books and plays as plots for movies, but it was not adequate. The M.P.P.D.A. under the leadership of Martin Quigley, a Catholic layman and publisher of motion picture trade papers adopted the Code in 1930 and it remained essentially the same ever since. Although parts have been clarified or slightly changed, the last modification dated from December 1955, and the new revised Motion Picture Code Production was published in December 1956 as result of it. The Association was in the beginning called the Hays Office after President Will H. Hays, a member of President Coolidge's Cabinet. A seal of approval was created and fines were established as a result of the Legion of Decency Campaign in 1934. The M.P.A.A. is composed of 21 permanent members representing almost the entire industry in this country (with the Board of Directors composed of 25 people from the industry and with the officers of Motion Picture Associations of America Inc., including 9 officers whose president for several years has been Eric Johnston, ex-member of Franklin Roosevelt's Administration, and on many occasions, Truman's and Eisenhower's special ambassador on delicate missions, controlled the whole movie industry directly and indirectly. On many occasions this organization not only controls domestic pictures but exercises a pressure on most of the world's production, directly or indirectly, having their offices in almost every major capital in the world, with the exception of the countries behind the "Iron Curtain."

The motion picture Code, which is one of many of the arms of the M.P.A.A., has served as a guide to the studios in avoiding material which might bring forth boycotts or censorship. Also it served the good intentions of the movie makers to the public—to receive complaints and to explain and defend the kind of movies which bear the code seal of approval.

The motion picture Code, in comparison to the newspaper Code, is essentially negative. Paying little attention to positive ideals of performance, it lays down a number of general and specific prohibitions and says in effect that these things do not constitute ethical conduct. Ethical conduct consists of what the drafters of the code believed to be public standards of morality. The movie Code emphasizes public morals; the newspaper Code—the public good. The ethical movie maker in general, will deplore sin and respect patriotism in his productions. Some sins, the Code observes, are inherently repellent, murder and cruelty for example. But others like sex and crimes of apparent heroism tend to attract. The latter needs more "care in treatment."

Let us analyse in more detail the new version of the Motion Picture Production Code. It is divided into 12 sections. The foreword stating that motion producers recognize the high trust and confidence which have been placed in them by the people of the world, which in turn has made motion pictures a universal form of entertainment. Hence, though regarding motion pictures primarily as entertainment without any explicit purpose of teaching or propaganda, they know that the motion picture within its own field of entertainment may be directly responsible for spiritual or moral progress, for higher types of social life and for much correct thinking.

On their part, the movie producers ask from the public and from public leaders a sympathetic understanding of the problems inherent in motion picture production and a spirit of cooperation that will allow the opportunity necessary to bring the motion picture to a still higher level of wholesome entertainment for all concerned. It states its general principles that no picture shall be produced which will lower the moral standards of those who see it. Hence, the sympathy of the audience shall never be thrown to the side of crime, wrong-doing, evil or sin. Correct standards of life, subject only to the requirements of drama and entertainment, shall be presented. Law, divine, natural or human shall not be ridiculed nor shall sympathy be created for its violation.

In Section 1 it is mentioned that crime shall never be presented in such a way as to throw sympathy with crime against law and justice or to inspire others with a desire for imitation. In Section 2 the emphasis is on brutality—that excessive and inhuman acts of cruelty and brutality shall not be presented. This includes all detailed and protracted presentation of physical violence, torture and abuse. In Section

3—sex, the sancity of the institution of marriage and the home shall be upheld. No film shall infer that causal or promiscuous sex relationships are the accepted or common thing. Lustful and open-mouth kissing, embraces, suggestive posture and gestures are not to be shown. In the same section under seduction and rape, these should never be more than suggested and then only when essential to the plot. The subject of abortion shall be discouraged, shall never be more than suggested and when referred to shall be condemned. The methods and techniques of prostitution and white slavery shall never be presented in detail. Brothels in any clear identification as such may not be shown. Sex perversion or any inference of it is forbidden. Sex hygiene and venereal diseases are not acceptable subject matter for theatrical motion pictures. Children's sex organs are never to be exposed, with the exception of infants.

In Section 4 under vulgarity such words as chippie, fairy, goose, nuts, pansy, S.O.B., etc., should be eliminated. The treatment of low, disgusting, unpleasant, though not necessarily evil, subjects should be guided always by the dictates of good taste and a proper regard for the sensitivities of the audience.

In Section 5—dances suggesting or representing sexual actions or emphasizing indecent movements are to be regarded as obscene.

In Section 6, blasphemy and profanity are forbidden, references to God, Lord, Jesus, Christ shall not be irreverent. The words "hell" and "damn", while sometimes dramatically valid, will be, if used without moderation, considered offensive by many members of the audience.

In Section 7 complete nudity, in fact or silhouette, is never permitted nor shall there be any licentious notice by characters in the film suggesting nudity. Indecent or undue exposure is forbidden.

In Section 8, on religion, no film or episode shall throw ridicule on any religious faith. Ceremonies of any definite religion shall be carefully and respectfully handled.

In Section 9 the use of the flag shall be consistently respectful; no picture shall be produced that tends to incite bigotry
or hatred among peoples of differing races, religions or national origins. The use of such offensive words as Chink, Dago,
Greaser, Hunkie, Kike, Nigger, Spic, Wop, Yid, Goon, should
be avoided.

Section 11 states the following titles shall not be used:
titles which are salacious, indecent, obscene, profane or vulgar.

Section 12 is dedicated to cruelty to animals, where it says
in the production of motion pictures involving animals, the
producer shall consult with authorized representative of the
American Humane Association and invite him to be present
during the staging of such animal action. There shall be no
use of any contrivance or apparatus for tripping or otherwise
treating animals in any unacceptably harsh manner. Hence, in
analyzing the Code, I have taken only as an example the most
important laws of the section.

Let us examine the other censorship—that by the government, which differs almost in every state where censorship is
practiced. Assuming that decisions of the U.S. Supreme Court
and other courts, since 1952, have not killed all motion picture
censorship explicitly and undeniably, neverthless it is clear
to all that serious constitutional doubts have been raised concerning the methods still being employed today in the states of
New York, Virginia, Maryland and Kansas as well as in several
municipalities. Among the states which still have censorship,
one of the most dreaded is of New York State.

Let us examine in detail what is called "Law, Rules and
Regulations for Review and Licensing of Motion Pictures"
under the auspices of the University of the State of New
York, the State Education Department governed by the Board
of Regents appointed and presided by the President of the
University and Commissioner of Education, whose director
of Division of Motion Pictures is at present Louis M. Pesce.
The motion picture Commission was originally created by an
act of the Legislature known as Chapter 715 of the Laws of

1921. This Commission functioned until January, 1927, when under the provisions of the State Department Law the activities of this Commission were transferred to the State Education Department. A Division of Motion Pictures was created and the Board of Regents was authorized to assign all the powers, duties and functions of the aforesaid Commission. The State Education Law was amended by Chapter 153 of the Laws of 1927, and a new article 43 was added. Chapter 820 of the Laws of 1947 revised the entire Education Law. Former article 43 became part 11 of article 3. Part 11 of this article as amended by Chapter 620 of the Laws of 1954, effective April 12, 1954, and in use at the present time.

The Director of the Division and the officers of a local office shall examine every motion picture film submitted to them, and unless such film or a part is obscene, indecent, immoral, inhuman, sacrilegious or is of such character that its exhibition would tend to corrupt morals or incite to crime, shall issue a licence therefor. If such director or officer will not license any film submitted, he will furnish to the applicant a written report of the reasons for his refusal and a description of each rejected part of a film not rejected in toto.

Paragraph 123 describes the "permits" for the "current event" films. All films exclusively, portraying current events or pictorial news of the day or excerpts from the public press, may be exhibited without inspection and no permits or fees are required.

Paragraph 125 states that permits are revocable. Any permit issued as provided in part 2 of this article or as provided in chapter 715 of the laws of 1921 may be revoked by such director or officer authorized to issue the same. Five days notice in writing is mailed to the applicant at the address named in the application.

Paragraph 129 describes unlawful use or exhibition. It shall be unlawful to exhibit or to sell, lease or lend for exhibition at any place of amusement for pay in connection with any business in the State of New York any motion picture film, other than those specified in subdivision 1 of Section 123, unless there is at the time in full force and effect a valid license or permit therefore from the Education Department.

Paragraph 130 is concerned with posters, banners, etc. No person or corporation shall exhibit or offer to another for exhibition purposes any poster or other similar advertising matter in connection with any motion picture film, which is obscene, indecent, immoral, inhuman or of such a character that its exhibition would tend to corrupt morals or incite to crime. If such poster, banner, etc., is so exhibited or offered to another for exhibition it shall be sufficient ground for the revocation of any permit or license issued by the Education Department.

Paragraph 131 disposes of the penalty. A violation of any provision of part 2 of this article shall be considered a misdemeanor. It also tells us about enforcement, rules and regulations. The Board of Regents shall have the authority to enforce the provisions and purposes of part 2 of this article, but this shall not be construed to relieve any State or local peace officer from the duty otherwise imposed of detecting and prosecuting violations of the laws of the State of New York. In carrying out and enforcing the purposes of part 2 of this article, the regents may make all needful rules and regulations. Article 16 disposes of the rules of the Board of Regents.

Paragraph 214—Examination of motion pictures. All motion pictures to be released within the State of New York for exhibition at any place of amusement for pay or in connection with any business shall be presented to the Motion Picture Division for examination at such times and places as the Division may designate. In the same paragraph under part 4, whenever the title of any motion picture appears on the film in foreign script or characters only, a title shall be added in English. Such title may consist of a phonetic rendering into English of the foreign language title.

Paragraph 216 of the Article 16 describes the procedure of eliminations or rejections—re-examination. If eliminations are directed by the Division to be made in any motion picture are rejected in toto by the Division, prompt notice of such eliminations or rejections shall be given to the applicant. Within five days after receipt of such notice the applicant has the right to file a request for re-examination of such motion picture and at such re-examination he will be advised of the decision made by the Director or his representative.

Paragraph 218 gives the right to any officer of the Division to enter and examine any theater or place of amusement where motion pictures are exhibited or where a motion picture is exhibited for amusement in connection with a business.

Paragraph 220 describes when the license or permit should be refused in certain cases. No motion picture shall be licensed or a permit granted for its exhibition within the State of New York, the whole or any part of which is obscene, indecent, immoral, inhuman or of such a character that its exhibition would tend to corrupt morals or incite to crime. It will denote a motion picture film or part, where the dominant purpose or effect of which is erotic or pornographic or portrays acts of sexual immorality, perversion or lewdness, etc. The "incite to crime" shall denote a motion picture the dominant purpose or affect of which is to suggest criminal acts or contempt for law which is profitable, desirable, acceptable or which advocates or teaches the use of or the methods of use of narcotics or habit-forming drugs.

Furthermore, the director or authorised officer shall collect from each applicant for a license permit, a fee of three dollars for each one thousand feet or fraction of original film and two dollars for each additional copy. The revocation or cancellation of any license or permit issued shall not entitle the grantee to the return of any fee paid.

Those 2 articles with their paragraphs mentioned here are the most important in the machine of censorship in the State of New York. If we analyze the motion picture code of in-

dustry and the ones of the governments we shall see principally
that paragraphs 122 and 220 are almost the same, but stated
with different words in the industry code. One can realize
that the self-imposed code of the producers is much more
restricted than the official one, and normally once it is approved by the M.P.A.A., it should be automatically approved
by the State regulation. In practice, however, this is not always
true. Since both types of regulations are very elastic and depend
on their interpretations, on several occasions a film approved
by M.P.A.A. was bound locally through the pressure of
religious groups, the views of the local censor, and of political
groups, and the courts were forced to decide on the issue.

In 1952 the unrealistic doctrine, which denied to motion
pictures the protection accorded to speech and the press,
received its long overdue *coup de grace* in the Burstyn vs.
Wilson, a case that involved the censorship of an Italian picture called "The Miracle", where the Legion of Decency boy-
cotted and forced the censor to ban the film on the ground
that it was sacrilegious. The U. S. Supreme Court reversed the
ban, and, at the same time, emphasized the narrow area open
to prior restraints. The Court decided without qualification
that "expression by means of motion picture is included within
the free speech and free press guaranty of the First and
Fourteenth Amendments".

The same law was also applied in another film banned by
the New York censor in the French picture "La Ronde" where
the court ruled that his picture cannot be censored on the
grounds of immorality. The Court also reversed Ohio's ban
on the film "M" on the grounds of "tending to promote crime"
and Texas' ban of the film "Pinky" on the grounds of inciting
racial tension. It is worth while to quote the decision in this
case of Justice Douglas, while these decisions were delivered
without opinion, it is worth noting the clear-cut language
employed in two concurrent cases. Referring to "Pinky" the
evil of prior restraint is present here in flagrant form. If Board
of Censors can tell the American public what it is in their

best interests to see, read or hear . . . "this regimented authority substituted for liberty and the great purpose of the First Amendment to keep uncontrolled the freedom of expressions defeated".

In another case involving two bans by New York and Ohio, the same judge stated "The First and Fourteenth Amendments say that Congress and the states shall make no law which abridges freedom of speech or of the press". In order to sanction a system of censorship per se and that it is now impossible for a censorship statute to be validly drafted.

Before we finish with the section of motion pictures, let us describe the pressure groups. In the MPAA, itself, we have an organization known as FEBNO, which is a kind of censorship in itself, which begins to function fully once the film is released to the public. The Film Estimate Board of National Organizations which cooperates between the industry and public spirited representatives of 13 American national organizations, among them we have the American Association of University Women, American Jewish Committee, American Library Association, National Council of Women, National Society Daughters of the American Revolution, National Congress of Parents and Teachers, School Motion Picture Committee, etc., known also by many as women censorship groups, where in very small proportion men are also represented. This organization is primarily interested in rating the pictures which are not suitable for young people or entire family, others for adult classification. Some of the films which receive adult classifications, which in most cases are the lowest, frequently condemn the picture and at times some of the members together with other groups form a direct pressure on a local censor, or even force the producer not to release the picture, or if once released to stop it. The FEBNO distributes gratis a "Green Sheet" known as "Joint Estimates of Current Entertainment Films" twice monthly which covers over 3,000,000 people mostly at secondary schools, libraries, colleges, etc. In addition most of the organizations disseminate their individual reviews to their own membership via such publications as: National Parent-Teacher Magazine, The Library Journal, The Christian Herald, etc. FEBNO audience suitability ratings are carried in screen stories, in various trade papers and in local newspapers throughout the country.

Another organization, very similar in its purpose, is the Legion of Decency run by the Catholic Church. It gives its opinion through its leaflets, but when the picture disagrees in any way with their ideals of the organization or the principles of the Catholic faith, directly or indirectly, they boycott it openly, and sometimes even with the help of the Churches as well. Their leaflets are published and graded in accordance with the view of their moral acceptability. As somebody says, a grading of "B" means morally objectionable in part or in general, is regarded by most of the industry as not serious but the "C" from the Legion, meaning "condemned" frightens the industry. This rating threatens organized boycott among Catholics and at times additional pressure is exercised by Catholic groups to pass restrictive legislation, to sharpen the teeth of state or municipal censorship. Let me quote the example of a picture "Forever Amber" which was given a "C" rating by the Legion of Decency. As the result of which Cardinal Spellman declared in a letter to all Pastors in his Diocese, which was read at Masses: "I advise the Catholics not to see the production with a safe conscience". Cardinal Dougherty in Philadelphia gave an ultimatum to the Fox Theater to withdraw the film within 48 hours or be faced with boycott. The studio cut and revised the film in consultation with the Legion and then made a public apology. The picture's rating was changed to "B" and everybody was happy.

The chief weapon of the pressure groups against the industry is the threat, implicit or explicit. Among other groups we can mention the Chamber of Commerce, the American Legion, all kinds of unions, syndicates or even community

Artistic and aesthetic value in a motion picture can be greatly hampered or destroyed by censorship.

PTA or any congregation may and sometimes does put the pressure on the industry to show a better quality picture. Most of the time, the same groups more or less organized make pressures on the legislator through hearings or other methods when the law in question is to be passed or debatable, show their strength, by what I would call "the unofficial censorship" which sometimes is the most effective.

The only trouble is that most censors don't know too much about the censorship of motion pictures, also the lacking of the elementary backgrounds of human psychology and have insufficient knowledge of law plus a complete disregard for what is known, in many countries, as "the science of filmology". This is a big handicap for the censors, and as a result the public and the producer suffer or are victims of this sad situation.

To our knowledge, the best censorship would be exercised by the pressure group itself, provided the people who will take this task will be adequately prepared for this kind of a job, on which the future of our children and our social order may depend. Unfortunately, the present organized or semi-organized pressure groups described above have even less background and preparation than the official censors themselves. A big help sometimes, are the critics of motion pictures such as Bosley Crowther, John McCarten, Archer Winsten, Wanda Hale, Abraham Weiler, Vincent Curby, Paul Buckley, Eugene Archer, Dorothy Masters, Leo Mushkin, Arthur Knight, Justin Gilbert, Nune Lagny, Alton Cook and others who through their respective papers criticise and grade pictures. In many cases, they make up the mind of the viewer whether to see particular pictures, and stimulate the producer to make better quality films. The motion picture is primarily a form of entertainment. Because of this the motion picture industry depends on the customers for the quality of films they want to see.

EPILOGUE

Throughout this book I have scrupulously tried to observe maximum objectivity in presenting only the opinions of others and not myself. Nonetheless, I daresay that it is impossible for any critic to steer clear of his own biases and prejudices. An opinion from the author may be useful to some readers. And, after recently viewing *Les Liaisons Dangereuses* and *La Dolce Vita*, I feel compelled to draw certain conclusions concerning the state of our contemporary cinema and of censorship. I have always been a strong partisan of intellectual freedom, and particularly of the artist's right to express himself freely. I have on many occasions and in many countries condemned, as a professional critic, the traditional heavy-handedness, ignorance and cynicism of censorship.

La Dolce Vita finds itself bordering between art and pornography, perhaps favoring the former. There is no doubt that *Les Liaisons Dangereuses* exceeds social definitions of decency. It is one thing for an artist to base his theme upon a couple's amorous peccadillos; it is quite another, however, for him to portray in the most attractive and exciting manner the gamut of sadistic adulterous behavior as in *Les Liaisons Dangereuses*. In such films, it does not suffice to exorcise individual scenes of obvious thread obscenity. The pernicious is interwoven inextricably throughout the entire fabric of the film, its settings, its characterizations and dialogue.

My objection to this kind of pornography does not stem from any formal religious or legal pretext. My objection to *Les Liaisons Dangereuses* is that it violates, distorts and mocks the very life principle. Even in the atheistic culture of the Soviet Union, there is a respect for the sanctity of married life and procreation. In this film, the producer has aimed for and attained the nadir in the degradation of woman. I think this nadir was reached when the diplomat employed the naked buttocks of his mistress as a base for the telephone while he described to his wife on the other end his sensations between bouts of love-making, to the relish and applause of his wife.

La Dolce Vita is doubtful family fare at best; but *Les Liaisons Dangereuses* under no circumstances should be exhibited to general public. One must doubt the wisdom of the French government in lifting its export ban on the film after three years of happy quarantine. Its exhibition abroad will not enhance the foreign public's image of the French people. It is imperative that the public be protected against the depravity of greedy producers who thrive on the exploitation of human weaknesses and by public I mean adults as well as children. However, there is nothing more self-defeating than unenlightened, inexpert censorship. Censorship groups should seek out wherever possible the help of psychiatrists, artists and filmologists to complement the traditional elderly gentlewomen, police officials, politicians and professional grouches.

I would like to suggest that UNESCO consider the establishment of an international censorship advisory council to help member nations control, on an enlightened basis, the public exhibition of obscenity, depravity and other anti-social manifestations. This would certainly contribute, in a major way, to relieving courts, mental institutions, and law enforcement officials around the world of their pathetic burdens.

We have nothing to lose but our neuroses.

BIBLIOGRAPHY

AMERICAN

1. The Film as Art—Museum of Modern Art Film Library, 1941—N.Y.C.
2. From Caligari to Hitler—S. Krakauer, Princeton 1947
   The Public Arts—Gilbert Seldes—Simon & Schuster, 1956 N.Y.C.
3. Case History of a Movie—Dore Schary—Random House— 1950. N.Y.C.
4. Movies—Psychological Study—by M. Wolfenstein and N. Leites, Free Press—1950—Chicago
5. Television and Education in the U.S.—by Charles A. Siepmann UNESCO—Paris, 1952
6. The Public is Never Wrong—1953—Zukor and Krammer— Putnam—N.Y.C.
7. The Techniques of Film Editing—Karel Reisz—Farrar, Strauss & Young—1953—New York
8. Atlantic Monthly—Supplement on Brazil 1956—Intercultural Publications, Inc—N.Y.C.
9. Motion Picture Associations of America, Inc. Publications 1955/56
10. Film Form and Film Sense—by Sergei Eisenstein 1957 Meridian Books, N.Y.
11. The Movies—by Richard Griffith and Arthur Meyer—1957— Simon & Schuster—N.Y.C.
12. Film as Art—R. Arnheim—University of Cal. Press—1957
13. The Lion's Share—by Bosley Crowther —Dutton 1957— N.Y.C.
14. Agee on Film—J. Agee—1958—McDowell, Obolensky— N.Y.C.
15. Film Culture—Magazine—1958/9/60—New York
16. Film in Review edited by Henry Holt, N.Y.C. 1957/8/9/60
17. Film: An Anthology—by Daniel Talbot and others—Simon & Schuster 1959—N.Y.C.
18. Classics of the Silent Screen—Joe Franklin etc. Citadel Press— N.Y. 1959
19. Variety Magazine—1958/9/60
20. Hollywood Rajah—by Bosley Crowther—Henry Holt & Rinehart & Winston—1960 N.Y.C.
21. Film Daily Year Book of Motion Pictures—Film Daily—N.Y.C.

22. International Motion Picture Almanac, Quigley Publications, N.Y.C.
23. The Liveliest Art—Arthur Knight—1959 Macmillan Co.—N.Y.C.
24. New Screen Techniques—Martin Quigley Jr. & others—1953 Quigley Publications, N.Y.C.
25. The Making of Public Opinion by Emory S. Bogardus, Association Press, New York, 1951
26. The Process & Effects of Mass Communications by William Schramm, University of Illinois Press, Urbana, 1954
27. Communications in Modern Society by Wilbur Schramm, 1948, University of Illinois Press
28. Mass Communication—T.V. Radio, Film, Press, by Eric Barnouv, Rinehart & Co. N.Y.C. 1956
29. The People's Right to Know—by H. J. Cross—Columbia University Press, 1953 N.Y.C.
30. The Great Audience—by Gilbert Seldes—The Viking Press, 1950 N.Y.C.
31. Freedom of the Press—by William L. Chenery, Harcourt & Brace, 1955 N.Y.C.
32. Hollywood Looks at its Audience—L. A. Handel, 1950—The Un. of Ill. Press—Ill.
33. The Rise of the American Film—Jacob Lewis, Harcourt-Brace, 1939—N.Y.C.
34. Film and its Techniques—Raymond Spottiswoode, University of California, 1951—Los Angeles
35. Freedom of the Movies—Ruth Inglis, University of Chicago, 1947
36. America at the Movies—Margaret F. Thorp, Yale University, 1939
37. Seen Any Good Movies Lately?—W. K. Zinsser, Doubleday, 1958, N.Y.C.
38. Movies, Morals and Art—F. Getlein & H. C. Gardiner, Sheed & Ward, 1961, N.Y.C.
39. The Image Industries—William F. Lynch, Sheed & Ward, 1959, N.Y.C.
40. The Fifty Year Decline and Fall of Hollywood, Ezra Goodman, Simon & Shuster, 1960. N.Y.C.

ENGLISH

1. Sociology of the Film—J. P. Mayer, 1946—London
2. The Cinema and the Public—by K. Box—London—1946

3. The Film—Roger Manwell—Pelican Books Edition, 1946— London
4. The Art of the Film—E. Lindgren—Allen & Unwin—1948 —London
5. Documentary Film—Paul Rotha—Faber & Faber—1952— London
6. British Magazine: Sight and Sound 1953/4/5—London
7. The Film and the Public—Roger Manvell, Penguin Publ. 1959 London
8. Children in the Cinema—Richard Ford, 1939 London
9. The Film Answers Back—E. W. Robson & M. M., John Lane— 1939 London
10. The Italian Cinema—V. Jaratt, Falcon Press, London 1951
11. Fifty Years of German Film—H. H. Wollenberg, Falcon Press 1947
12. Soviet Cinema—T. Dickinson and C. de la Roche, Falcon Press 1948

PORTUGUESE

1. Principio e Fim do Nazismo—C. Vilar—Edition Atlantica— 1952—Rio de Janeiro
2. O Gangster no Cinema—S. Cavalcanti de Paiva—Andes Edition—Rio de Janeiro—1953
3. Filme e Realidade—by Alberto Cavalcanti—Edition Martins— 1953—São Paulo, Brazil
4. Congress of Criminology—1954—São Paulo—Brazil (my participation)
5. Pequena Historia do Cinema Brasileiro—by Silva Nobre 1955— Rio de Janeiro, Private Publ.
6. Cinema e Criança—Mark Koenigil—1955—São Paulo, Brazil —Edition Iris
7. Cinema Brasileiro Como Industria e Relaçoes Publicas by Mark Koenigil, 1956—Theses-project—Brazilian Congress—Rio de Janeiro
8. Brazilian Motion Picture Congress Library—1953/55/56
9. Significão de Far West—Otavio de Faria, Rio de Janeiro, 1952
10. Cartilha de Cinema—Carlos Ortiz—Editorial Iris, São Paulo, 1949
11. Noçoes de Cinema—Bonifacio Fortes, Aracaju, 1953, Brasil
12. Magazine "Elite" Special Edition of the São Paulo International Festival of the Cinema, February 1954, Brasil
13. Primeira Mostra do Cinema Brasileiro—São Paulo, 1952

FRENCH

1. Le Film Recreatif pour Spectateurs Juveniles—Henry Storck, UNESCO, Paris 1950
2. Cas Difficiles—J. de Buch, Edition D.D.B. 1942—Paris
3. Le Cinema, Notre Metier—Eyder, Rossay, etc. Skira Ed. 1946 Paris
4. De Muet au Parlant—A. Arnoux—La Nouvelle Edition 1946— Paris
5. Congress of Criminologie, Sorbonne, Paris 1950 (my participation)
6. International Congress of Mental Medicine 1951—Vevey— (Switzerland)
7. Le Courrieur—Volume 4—1951—UNESCO Publication—Paris
8. L'Enfant en Proie aux Images—by Armand Lanoux—Labergerie Edition—1951—Paris
9. Revue d'Educateur—Connsaisance de Cinema—1951/52—Paris
10. Le Cinema a-t-il une Ame—Angel, 1952—Paris
11. Revue Internationale de Filmologie—1951/2/3—Presses Universitaire de France, Paris
12. Derriere l'Ecran—J. P. Chartier and R. P. Desplanques—Spes Publication 1953—Paris
13. French Film—by Georges Sadoul—Falcon Press, Paris—1953
14. Étude de Marche du Cinema Français—by Centre National de la Cinematographie, 1954—Paris

INDIAN

1. The Indian Film—Panna Shah—The Motion Picture Society of India, Bombay, 1950
2. Indian Film Industry—S. H. Booch—India Information Services—New Delhi, 1954

ITALIAN

1. Revue Bianco e Nero—Collection 1952/3/4—Edition Dell Atene, Rome, Italy
2. Gli Intellectuali e il Cinema—M. Verdoni, 1952, Rome

INDEX

211